The Church Confident

Leander E. Keck

Abingdon Press
Nashville

THE CHURCH CONFIDENT

Copyright © 1993 by Abingdon Press

This book is printed on recycled, acid-free paper.

Library of Congress Cataloging-in-Publication Data

Keck, Leander E.
   The church confident / Leander E. Keck.
      p.   cm.
   Includes bibliographical references.
   ISBN 0-687-08151-3 (alk. paper)
      1. Protestant churches—United States.   2. Church renewal—United States. 3. United States—Church history—20th century.   I. Title.
   BR526.K443   1993
   280'.4'097309049—dc20   92-33161
                                                                      CIP

Scripture quotations, except for brief paraphrases or unless otherwise noted, are from the New Revised Standard Version Bible, copyright 1989, by the Division of Christian Education of the National Council of the Churches of Christ in the United States of America. Used by permission.

93 94 95 96 97 98 99 00 01 02 — 10 9 8 7 6 5 4 3 2 1

MANUFACTURED IN THE UNITED STATES OF AMERICA

FOR JAN

CONTENTS

FOREWORD

Customary courtesy calls for saying something about persons being introduced; so too, it is proper to provide some information about a book being introduced to readers.

The Church Confident contains the Lyman Beecher Lectures given at Yale Divinity School in February 1992 on the theme "Toward the Renewal of Mainline Protestantism." Although the Beecher Lectures, begun in 1871, have traditionally dealt with preaching, in recent years the scope has been broadened to include other aspects of Christian ministry as well. Since much of what I have to say about preaching is found in my *Bible in the Pulpit* (Abingdon, 1978), the current flexibility of the Beecher Lectures permits me to address the state of "mainline" Protestantism and aspects of its renewal.

For a number of years, the Beecher Lectures have consisted of four presentations, given during the annual Winter Convocation. Dealing with the dilemma and renewal of the "mainline" churches' life in four lectures required identifying those aspects of their life that are central; any one of them could easily be developed into four presentations. For various reasons, it seemed prudent to publish the lectures largely as given, with minor revisions, and occasional expansions. The footnotes give the material more texture and somewhat wider horizons.

Many aspects of the current situation of the "mainline" also plague other segments of Protestantism, and to some extent Catholicism, as well. Indeed, a comparable volume needs to be written about evangelical and charismatic parts of the Protestant family. That task, however, must go to someone else. My task in these lectures was to discuss what had led to the current malaise in a significant strand of Protestantism, and to say a word that might contribute to overcoming its current entropy. Judiciously balanced generalizations, like adequate comprehensiveness, must be left for historians of American Christianity, whose lot it is not only to include all parts of the story but also to account for their relative importance on the national scene. My task called for a more focused, and more critical, stance.

These lectures would have been given in 1991 had not a serious auto accident occurred a week before Convocation. I want to record my gratitude to four colleagues who, on very short notice, each presented a lecture on that occasion: David Bartlett, Brevard Childs, Margaret Farley, and Abraham Malherbe. The one-year delay did, of course, permit me to re-write all the lectures yet another time.

Following the completion of two five-year terms as Dean of Yale Divinity School, I was determined to use a leave of absence in 1989–1990 to revise for publication the Shaffer Lectures on New Testament Christology, given at Yale in 1980. In order to work as well on the Beecher Lectures, the Lilly Endowment provided funds that made it possible to be released from teaching duties also in the fall semester of 1990 and undergirded the costs of research and manuscript preparation work as well. Without this support and encouragement for which I am deeply grateful, this project would not have been brought to completion.

In the struggle to discern the substance of these lectures and to give it shape, I have benefited enormously from conversations with colleagues too numerous to record here. I must, however, mention one colleague and friend of more than four decades, J. Louis Martyn, who read an earlier draft of the lectures and responded with both penetrating criticism and steady encouragement to continue. Above all, I am grateful for the trenchant critiques and unfailing support from my two sons, Stephen and David, both completing their doctoral studies as historians (at Oxford and Harvard, respectively), but perceptive theologians as well. Unfortunately, no tape recorder preserves the lively exchanges of our nocturnal seminars. It is they and their generation who have the most at stake in the possible renewal of "mainline" Protestantism. They understand why, nonetheless, this book is dedicated to their mother.

Holy Week, 1992

PRELIMINARY REMARKS
ABOUT PERSPECTIVE

It is impossible to be a Christian. It is impossible not to be a Christian. It is impossible to be a Christian outside the Church and the Church is impossible.

—Petru Dumitriu, *To the Unknown God*

Seeking God with one's whole heart is no joke, especially if it might be the only way to find him.

—Paul L. Holmer, *The Grammar of Faith*

Personal Musings

I want to begin with a few preliminary remarks of a personal sort because I am keenly aware that there is something incongruous about my giving the Lyman Beecher Lectures, and especially about this topic, even though I have spent more than three decades trying to educate the future leaders of the churches, spoken to more pastors' schools than I can recall, and preached in churches and chapels of all sorts.

First, I am not a birthright mainliner, but one who has adopted this part of the Christian church. I grew up in what used to be called the German Baptist General Conference (now the North American Baptist Conference), then made up largely of Germans who had immigrated from Eastern Europe and Russia. Schwäbisch German was in fact my native language; I learned English the summer before starting school. My earliest memories of church go back to the white frame building on the North Dakota prairie, and include getting there by horse and sleigh, with a stop at Grandpa's house to reheat the rocks that kept our feet warm. After moving to western Washington during the Depression, we again found a German Baptist church, one that gradually made the transition to English during my youth. It was during undergraduate days that I began my migration out of this tradition, first into the American Baptist Convention while at Andover Newton, and then, while in Nashville, into the Disciples of Christ. In making these moves, I have not gone as a rebel or a refugee, but as one seeking, and finding, wider access to the fullness of the Christian tradition. Being an outsider to the mainline for the first and formative part of my life probably conditioned my outlook once I moved to the inside.

In the second place, there is something incongruous about a Beecher lecturer with ambivalence toward the mainline churches. This reflects neither regret nor guilt for moving away from my patrimony, but rather it stems from harboring dual impulses of loyalty and disaffection. My loyalty to the church is probably irradicable, because I have been involved with a church all my life. Indeed, I regard those who have been preaching since puberty as latecomers, for I was preaching revival sermons to my pets before starting school and threatening the cats with baptism by immersion. But the sinners got away. For the first part of my life, I was in church twice every Sunday, and although I served as pastor only in an interim capacity, no aspect of the church's life remained foreign to me save the inner workings of the women's society. Quite simply, the church has been part of me for my entire life; I accepted "adult" baptism in a cold mountain stream at the ripe age of nine.

Nonetheless, I have found myself estranged from the churches that are so much a part of me. What put me off was not only that the continual tinkering with denominational machinery seemed to be diverting energy away from coherent witness and toward struggles for power, but also that confidence in the gospel, and in the grand vision of a Christian humanism, was being abandoned, it often seemed, in favor of either narcissistic spirituality or frenetic activity. The churches' identity and mission seemed to be determined less and less by the resources of the gospel and their tested wisdom and more and more by extraneous agendas. That their identity and mission always, and inevitably, were forged in interaction with their circumstances is a truism, but that "the world sets the agenda" is sheer capitulation. In turbulent decades, the heritage of precedents—the steely as well as the golden—was neglected, and plastic, trendy throwaways were improvised instead. The churches seemed to act like inheritors of an estate who camped in the yard because they neither knew nor cared how to live in the house.

Indeed, some authors of best-sellers for the religious market and religious leaders themselves were, in effect if not in intent, telling the churches not to live in the house. Repeatedly, church people were told that what their forebears had emphasized was of dubious value—faithful church attendance, dependable participation in its programs and charitable activities, and even "full-time Christian service" in the church's ministries—because "real Christians" were marching in the streets, sitting on various boards, or "going to Washington" (the activists' Vatican), since that was where the action was. In an era punctuated by assassinations of public figures and civil rights workers, by the burning of cities and draft cards, it was understandable that earnest and committed church leaders would insist that their constituents lay aside much of the accumulated trivia in order to respond constructively to the upheavals that society was experiencing simultaneously.

What such urging revealed, however, was how ill-prepared the churches were to deal with the crises of the times, for, apart from "Brotherhood" Sundays and the like, what many congregations had heard from their pulpits or learned in classrooms simply lacked sufficient theological protein to equip them for the ethical struggles. Had the theological warrants for social change been deeply rooted before, church folk might have been less resistant and more willing to follow; as it was, what the leadership could do was "to tell them what was wrong with them. They could not empower the laity to do what was right," as sociologist Benton Johnson observes. He also notes that the leaders "tried to build a fire under the laity by depriving them of the remaining landmarks of church life. In the process . . . they conveyed the impression that the churches are irrelevant to anything that matters in the world."[1]

---

1. Benton Johnson, "Is There Hope for Liberal Protestantism?" in a paper presented to the Council on Theological Education of the Presbyterian Church (U.S.A.) in 1986, printed in *Mainstream Protestantism in the Twentieth Century: Its Problems and Prospects,* p. 20.

As a teacher of New Testament to seminarians, I saw my vocation clearly: to put the future leaders of the churches in touch with those theological resources which could equip them to lead their people into the new era instead of flogging them into the future, and to help them think critically about the simplicities and rigidities of both the left and the right.

Feeling sometimes estranged from the mindset of many contemporaries is something I do not regard lightly or parade cavalierly. Whereas the apostle Paul was a Jew among Jews and a Greek among Greeks, I have often found myself a Jew among Greeks and a Greek among Jews, a conservative among liberals and a liberal among conservatives—not, I think, out of sheer contrariness but because I could never take for granted either the Christian faith or my relation to it.

Accordingly, it was not the churches' liberal posture in social and political matters that I found frustrating, for I often agreed with much of it, but the arrogant and self-righteous rhetoric which, in various ways, asserted that they knew exactly which changes in society were "where God is at work"—as if the reactionary right were not making much the same claim. Moreover, slogans and code words seemed to hide the absence of serious thought, and theology looked ever more like ideology for causes—a perversion as unacceptable when leaning leftward as when pointed to the right. For the most part, then, I have not deemed it my calling to add my fagot to fires already burning, or to say more loudly what is already being said—whether or not I agree with it.

The only justification for recording such matters here is the surmise that this ambivalence about the mainline churches has affected also my thinking about their possible renewal. Without my lifelong concern for the well-being of the churches, the topic would not have been chosen at all.

Yet, one cannot deal with it usefully without calling attention to what seems to have gone wrong. The intent, however, is not to use this occasion as an emetic with which to free myself of sundry frustrations but to suggest alternatives derived from the Christian faith's own capacity for renewing and sustaining the churches.

It would be gross faithlessness to assume that the Christian faith, itself repeatedly renewed by the gospel, now lacks the capacity to renew the churches—as if our situation were more effective in draining off the vitality of the faith than that of our predecessors. If renewal and reform have come about in the past, there is no persuasive reason to deny that they will occur again.

Indeed, I suspect that we are on the threshold of a new Christian sensibility, a different understanding of what counts in being Christian, a new pattern of piety and practice which reflects the unity of faith and ethics, a changed perception of what it means to be a faithful church. Should that materialize, it would come to pass as a result of renewal. That is why the plight of the church needs attention now.

The Malaise of the Mainline

Diagnosing the malaise of mainline Protestant churches and prescribing remedies has become a growth industry. Careers are being made, and perhaps unmade as well, by analyzing the disease and urging cures. The conviction is widespread that mainline Protestantism is in a crisis and that it cannot continue indefinitely on its present course. Perhaps the British historian Paul Johnson will prove to be right in suggesting that the current crisis of the mainliners is actually the birth pangs of the Fourth Great Awakening.[2] In any case, fine-tuning will not be enough; what is needed is not

---

2. Paul Johnson, "The Almost-Chosen People: Why America Is Different," in Neuhaus, *Unsecular America,* p. 13.

improvement but renewal that reforms the churches' worship, theology, ethos, and communication. Changes in these four,[3] taken together, can restore *the church confident*—a less abrasive image today than the earlier "church militant."[4] All four topics impinge on the ministry of preaching a renewing word to the mainline churches.

Admittedly, "mainline" is an ambiguous term. On the one hand, it is rather anachronistic, having come into use just when the remarkable growth of conservative, evangelical, and charismatic churches made it hard to decide who is mainline and who is sideline.[5] On the other hand, the word is sometimes used in a normative way (implying that these churches are the standard by which the others are to be measured), and sometimes in a pejorative sense (implying a somewhat specious form of Christianity).[6] The word will be used here to designate an uncommonly influential segment of American Protestantism, beginning with the Episcopalians, Congregationalists, and Presbyterians in colonial days, and then enlarged to encompass the growing role of Baptists, Campbellites, Lutherans, Methodists, and Reformed. Even today, their influence is greater than their numbers, for they make up only 10 percent of the population.[7]

---

3. These four agendas are, to some extent, comparable to Leonard Sweet's call for a reconstructed theology, a revised ecclesiology, a rehabilitated patriotism, and a reconstructed supernaturalism. "Can a Mainstream Change Its Course?" in Michaelson, *Liberal Protestantism*, p. 236.

4. Part of the difficulty with "church militant" is that in the minds of many it suggests cultural "triumphalism." Ironically, the image of the "church militant" has fallen into disfavor precisely at a time when Christians and churches understand themselves as engaged in "struggle" for social justice, and do not hesitate to be quite "militant" in doing so!

5. Roof and McKinney, *American Mainline Religion*, p. 74.

6. R. Laurence Moore contends that " 'mainline' has too often been misleadingly used to label what is 'normal' in American religious life and 'outsider' to characterize what is aberrational and not-yet American. In fact, the American religious system may be said to be 'working' only when it is producing novelty, even when it is fuelling antagonisms," *Religious Outsiders*, p. 208.

7. Roof and McKinney, *American Mainline Religion*, p. 87.

Wade Clark Roof and William McKinney's important book, *American Mainline Religion,* divides the mainliners into three groups on the basis of prevailing theological stance; the Episcopalians, Presbyterians, and United Church of Christ turn out to be "liberals," and the other five "moderates." Although any grouping of denominations according to theological perspectives is precarious, analyzing the plight of the mainline Protestant churches does entail assessing the role of liberal theology and its offspring, because while many factors contributed to the current state of affairs, this theology has become ever more influential in all of these churches and has provoked the rise of conservative caucuses within them. Controversies related to liberal theology are by no means new to these churches, but what distinguishes the current situation is their own suspicion that, as a religious movement, liberal Protestantism has spent itself, and is now an extinct volcano in whose crater all sorts of things now flourish.

The leading cause of this foreboding is the drastic decline in membership. Two litanies have rationalized this decline. On the one hand, it is said that the decline is not so great, because the earlier statistics were inflated. On the other hand, it is claimed that the churches are stronger and leaner, because their prophetic social witness has thinned the ranks. Although neither explanation is completely wrong, both finally are withered fig leaves unable to hide reality. Something is indeed amiss when a major denomination loses 245 members a day for more than twenty years, an aggregate of 2 million persons.[8] Nor is it irrelevant that for every person

---

8. Gerald Anderson, writing about The United Methodist Church in *Good News* (September-October 1990), p. 22. According to Leonard Sweet, the Church reported that in 1984 "42% of churches had no constituency rolls, 60% no confirmation or membership training classes, and 38% did not receive a single new member by profession of faith." "The Modernization of Protestant Religion in America," in Lotz, *Altered Landscapes,* pp. 39-40.

from a nonreligious background who joins a mainline church, three leave it for no church at all.[9] Most of them did not renounce the faith; indeed, they may well continue to be believers, perhaps more serious ones than some who remained, yet they simply drifted away. Demographically, the future growth of the churches greatly depends on the eighteen-year-olds to thirty-four-year-olds; however, the statistics gathered by Roof and McKinney show that the more liberal the church the less attractive it is to just this group.[10]

To be sure, many congregations do continue to grow, and there are indeed pastors whose lives and witness are faithful to the gospel and vigorous in helping their parishes live it, just as there are groups and places that are being renewed today. They deserve to be remembered and strengthened. Still, their existence may be the exception that proves the rule. Their continued vitality no more means that the mainliners as a whole are not in trouble than two healthy kidneys prove that a person is not sick.

The case for the entropy of mainline Protestantism does not need to be argued any more. What does need sober thought is whether that state can be reversed by renewal and reform. Renewal cannot be programmed. One cannot devise a clear sequence of steps that will guarantee renewal. The order in which we consider the topics does not provide a program, a sequence of measures for renewal; it simply reflects a certain logic—from identity to mission. We begin with worship because this goes to the heart of the matter.

---

9. Roof and McKinney, *American Mainline Religion*, p. 170.

10. Ibid., p. 153. The evidence shows that the more liberal groups (Episco-palians, Presbyterians, and UCC) attracted the smallest percentage of new members (on average 27 percent) from the total pool of eighteen-year-olds to thirty-four-year-olds.

CHAPTER ONE

WORSHIP

We express our delight in a beautiful or lovely thing no less by lament for its loss, than gladness in its presence, much art is therefore tragic or pensive, but all pure art is praise. . . . Fix, then, this in your mind . . . your art is to be praise of something that you love.

—John Ruskin, "The Laws of Fésole"

The praise of God is the most prominent and extended formulation of the *universal* and *conversionary* dimension of the theology of the Old Testament.

—Patrick D. Miller, *Interpretation* 39 (1985)

Christian liturgy should intensify the "cognitive dissonance" between the community of faith and the world surrounding it.

—Richard John Neuhaus, *The Catholic Moment*

The church sings praises not only toward God but [also] against the gods.

—Walter Brueggemann, *Israel's Praise*

Renewing any institution requires revitalizing its core, its reason for being. Unless this core is refocused and funded afresh, renewal becomes a matter of strategy for survival. Accordingly, the churches' renewal becomes possible only when their religious vitality is energized again by a basic reform of their worship of God. Worship enacts and proclaims a construal of Reality and of our relation to it. Aidan Kavanagh put it well: In liturgy the church "is caught in the act of being most overtly itself as it stands faithfully in the presence of the One who is both the object and the source of . . . faith."[1] To call for a reform in the worship of God, however, implies that the churches' standing before God is flawed seriously enough to require a turnabout, the biblical word for which is "repentance."

Is the situation really so serious? A cartoon illustrates the question: A man carrying a sandwich board on which huge letters demand, "Repent!" Near the bottom, in small print, the sentence: "If you have already repented please disregard this notice." Some people would indeed claim that many "mainline" churches have already "repented" of their inherited Protestant worship. Have they not turned to lectionaries, gotten the preacher out of an elevated pulpit and onto the floor with the congregation, adopted color-coded vestments and paraments, encouraged "experimental worship," and, like the seventh-inning stretch, stopped worship of God in order to shake hands, embrace, kiss, and chatter briefly under the rubric of "passing the peace"? Indeed they have, but in many cases it has amounted to little more than a substitution of the trivial for the ossified! Some changes have been deeper. The liturgical movement, for example, has helped congregations rediscover the rich resources of the church catholic, but many Protestant congregations remain only marginally affected by it.

---

1. Aidan Kavanagh, *On Liturgical Theology*, p. 75.

In any case, far too often, the "mainline" churches are indeed "caught in the act," engaged in worship which is thoroughly secularized. I recall an occasion when the traditional invocation was replaced with the rousing cheer for God: "Gimme a G; gimme an O; gimme a D!" An extreme example, to be sure, but nonetheless an example. There will be no renewal of mainline Protestantism until its worship of God is redeemed from such silliness and the secularization it reflects.[2] If the Australian historian is right in asserting that "secularization is a much deadlier foe than any previous counter-religious force in human experience,"[3] then one can see immediately what is at stake in the secularization of worship—the identity and integrity of the church as church, that

---

2. Few themes of North Atlantic history have been explored more diversely than the secularization of our culture. Clearly the primary meaning of secularization depends on the base line from which one gauges the change into secularity or worldliness. (a) If the base line is a sacred world, one inhabited by the sacred spirits, then secularization means desacralization—a process that transforms the world from a "thou" into an "it." Because this view makes religion and science alternatives, it has limited use in explaining why our highly advanced scientific-technological society continues to be quite religious. The complexity of this phenomenon is outlined by George M. Marsden ("Are Secularists the Threat? Is Religion the Solution?" in Neuhaus, *Unsecular America*, pp. 31-51). (b) If the base line is Christendom, then secularization means the steady dechristianization of our culture. But this implies that American culture was once pervasively Christian whereas according to Everett C. Ladd, "America is today what it has always been: a highly religious, intensely secular society" ("Secular and Religious America," in Neuhaus, *Unsecular America*, p. 23); moreover, the recent entry of conservative and fundamentalist churches into public affairs implies that Christian influence has actually increased (so Robert Wuthnow, *The Struggle for America's Soul*, p. 54).

More satisfactory is the view of Peter Berger: Since all views of reality attain their plausibility when the people who hold them are especially influential, the secular world view has come to prevail among the opinion-makers, the so-called new class—the scientists, academics, media folk, and others who manage the flow of information and ideas (Peter L. Berger, *Facing Up to Modernity*, p. 158). See also chap. 2, n. 14.

In light of these observations, we may regard secularization as a process in which a growing number of people find a religious sensibility irrelevant for their own thought and conduct, and basically harmless (though perhaps emotionally useful) for those who retain it, but who feel threatened when this sensibility "goes public."

3. Alan D. Gilbert, *The Making of Post-Christian Britain*, p. 153. Though he focused on the British experience, Gilbert's study is often suggestive for understanding the experience in North American Protestantism as well.

is, whether the church "stands faithfully in the presence of
the One who is both the object and the source of faith." And
the antidote to this secularization is restoring the integrity of
the center of worship—the praise of God.

The Praise of God

We use the word "praise" with respect to people and
things as well as with respect to God; so it is useful to
start by recalling *what praise is and does generally,* leav-
ing latent just now the application of praise to God. To
begin with, praise is an oral activity, whether in speech or
song, which acknowledges a superlative quality (like
patience or beauty), or a deed (like a heroic rescue). It is
more than an attitude of appreciation or an emotion like
delight, although it usually includes elements of both. As
verbal acknowledgment, praise is response to what we see
or experience. Praise does not express a yearning or wish
but responds to something given to us. The "bravos" at
the end of a brilliant concert, like the "Fantastic!" when a
Larry Bird arches a long shot through the hoop without
the ball touching the rim, are a response elicited by the
act itself. When praise acknowledges, it proclaims truth;
otherwise it is flattery and deceit, deceiving both the one
praised and the one doing the praising. We shall see that
the nexus between praise and truth is crucial for the task
of theology.

One can also respond negatively to people or things,
whether with envy or resentment, or with a put-down
("What's so great about that?") or outright denial of excellence ("Pure luck!"). Praise, however, reveals a positive
response to what or who is being praised.

Further, this positive relation implies that who or what
one praises is an important clue to one's character. The
object of praise reveals what one deems praiseworthy, what

we value and perhaps aspire to be like. But even if we do not aspire to sing like Pavarotti, in praising his rendition of a difficult solo we show that we value excellence. And whoever does not value excellence, especially if it is achieved by discipline, will not strive for it in one's own life. Whether by affirmation or by aspiration, the praised both reveals and shapes the praiser.

In the fourth place, grammatically, praise can use either second person or third person. We use the second person to address the person directly: "Your work is brilliant"; we use the third person to extol that excellence to others: "Her work is brilliant." Using the second person, speaking to the one praised, establishes or maintains a relationship; using the third person, speaking about the praised, invites others to share in the praise, and so generates and maintains community. Half the fun of being a sports enthusiast is finding out who else praises or blames the same players as you do.

Finally, although praise is not the result of weighing evidence judiciously but is usually a prompt and spontaneous response, it does reflect comparison. Otherwise, one would not know the difference between the excellent and the ordinary. But where does this capacity to discriminate and discern excellence come from? It is learned and warranted in a community of discourse, as in an antiques appraiser's ability to recognize and value a rare piece of Limoges porcelain, or a judge's ability to spot a superlative collie at a dog show. The acquired capacity manifests disciplined habits of seeing and valuing, which reflect the ethos of a knowledgeable community.[4]

These elemental observations about praise deserve to be

---

4. The emphasis on the importance of learning in a community comports well with Stanley Hauerwas's observation that learning Christianity is like learning a craft. "Discipleship as a Craft, Church as Disciplined Community," *The Christian Century* 108, no. 27 (October 2, 1991): 881-84.

amplified and nuanced; nonetheless, I trust that they suffice to allow us to consider more directly the praise of God.[5]

To begin with, there is a significant difference between praising a person and *praising God*. Syntactically, of course, there is no difference between saying, "Susan's kindness is outstanding," and saying "God's kindness is outstanding." Yet the content is not the same, because God and Susan belong to totally different categories, because God is not simply Susan in italics but the Ground of her existence. In praising Susan we acknowledge the excellence of a fellow creature; in praising God we acknowledge the excellence of her Creator, and ours as well.

We cannot take this acknowledgment for granted, because praising the Creator must contend successfully with alternative impulses, attitudes, and habits of thought. Only so can praising God emancipate us from the secularity that inhabits us. At precisely this point it becomes apparent that praising God is a discipline, a formative factor in the shape of our lives. Otherwise it becomes an occasional, sporadic exception to the rules, a flight from what we take to be reality instead of a sustained challenge to it.

For us creatures to praise the Creator is to acknowledge our contingency, a contingency that is more than the psychological state it tended to be for Schleiermacher, who spoke of the immediate feeling or sense *(Gefühl)* of dependence. Rather, this contingency is a built-in status to which we refer when we speak of God's transcendence. God's transcendence is not a matter of *distance* between heaven and earth but is one of ontic *difference*. In praising the transcendent God, we

---

5. The praise of God is, of course, the over-arching theme of the book of Psalms, in which the final psalm is unique because it calls to praise without giving a reason for doing so. Patrick D. Miller's explanation of this phenomenon is insightful: "Having called to praise and given the reason for praise throughout all the psalms, the Psalter now concludes . . . with a final straightforward call to praise. The psalm, therefore, is the 'Hallelujah' note for the whole book." "Enthroned on the Praises of Israel," *Interpretation* 39 (1985): 11 n. 9.

agree that H. Richard Niebuhr got it right in saying, "We are in the grip of power that neither asks our consent before it brings us into existence nor asks our agreement to continue us in being beyond our physical death."[6] To praise the Creator is to acknowledge joyously, not grudgingly, that we did not make ourselves but are contingent on the One who cannot and must not be reduced to the guarantor of our cultures and causes, however noble their aims and achievements. To praise the transcendent Creator is to acknowledge that it is not the divine Reality that is contingent on us, but we on it— an observation important in the next chapter.

In other words, authentic praise of God acknowledges what is true about God; it responds to qualities that are "there" and not simply "there for me." This is true generically of praise, not just of God-oriented praise. The person who praises an athlete's achievement, a work of art, the manifestation of a person's virtue, affirms that these are indeed praiseworthy, and that something would be wrong with a beholder who did not acknowledge them. In other words, God is to be praised because God is God, because of what God is and does, quite apart from what God is and does for me. Anyone can, and should, praise God when the Lord blesses one and keeps one, when the Lord makes his face to shine upon one and is gracious to one, when the Lord lifts up his countenance upon one and grants peace (Num. 6:24-26). Gratitude is indeed often expressed as praise, and rightly. But that does not make praise and gratitude identical. Or does God cease to be praiseworthy when gratitude has fled because the Lord seems to withhold blessing, when the divine face appears to be set against us, and when agony drives out peace? If God is indeed praiseworthy, must God earn our praise?

If this Reality is the Creator to whom we trace our exis-

---

6. H. Richard Niebuhr, *Faith on Earth,* p. 66.

tence but who does not trace its existence to us, then it has an integrity of its own, an integrity whose ways are not our ways, and whose ends cannot be conflated with ours. Only such a Reality is worthy of praise, inherently.

If these reflections are sound, one inference cannot be avoided: Since the Creator is praiseworthy, the creature has a moral obligation to acknowledge this with praise. Indeed, the apostle Paul regarded the refusal to do so—to honor God as God, as he put it—as the root cause of the human dilemma. Not that humanity withheld God-oriented praise categorically. Far from it. In Paul's words, people "exchanged the glory of the immortal God for images resembling a mortal human being or birds or fourfooted animals or reptiles" (Rom. 1:23). In other words, praise was directed toward the non-God as if it were God. Instead of inferring that the created is not the Creator, humanity *rei*fied the Creator and *dei*fied the creature, thereby exchanging truth for falsehood while claiming it was truth. As a result, everything else went wrong, and stays wrong until made right by God. It is not accidental that when Paul characterized the person whose God-relation was right, he said that "Abraham was strengthened in faith as he gave glory to God" (author's trans.)—or as he might have put it, "as he praised the truly praiseworthy God." Let no one think that for aged Abraham praising God, honoring God as God, was easy. The patriarch had to overcome his resistance based on the evidence of his and Sarah's age. And we have our own resistance as well. We cannot avoid facing it if the renewal of our worship turns on the praise of God.

The chief obstacle to praising God is the suffering that is not self-inflicted. Whether the innocent suffer because of natural disasters (like earthquakes) or because the consequences of human folly and injustice (like wars and revolutions) do not fall only on the guilty, the burden of suffering is so heavy that praising God seems not only out of the question but also a violation of our moral sense. And so we tacitly concede that the second-century heretic, Marcion, had a point: The God who created and rules this world is not praiseworthy, because God neither made a world that is disaster-proof nor arrests the consequences of our sins.

Still, in the mysterious ecology of joy and suffering, goodness and mercy can, and often do, appear even in suffering. Agony is not our only experience, though it readily overshadows the good that also comes our way. And just as we cannot explain all the suffering that is caused in pursuit of the good, so we cannot explain the coming of the good either. If we take the good for granted, we lose perspective also on the suffering that we must endure. Those who see only that the glass is half empty do not praise.

It would be as monstrous to require those whose lives are twisted by suffering to praise God as it would be to ask them to still their cries into the silence of heaven. Whoever did that must also tell the dying Jesus to stifle his "Eloi, Eloi, lema sabachthani?" That Luke did so by replacing this cry with a statement of exemplary piety should not tempt us away from the paradox of the Markan and Matthean reports, which invite us to affirm that God was present although not even Jesus could see it.[7]

The Christian community dares to praise the God who did not exempt Jesus from the agony of the cross but let him share undeserved suffering with us. This is the God who did not repudiate Jesus for hurling his Eloi heavenward and then dying with a primal scream. If God vindicated a man who died like this, we are assured that our own agonies need not

---

7. Matt. 27:46 follows the Markan report of Jesus' last words, taken from Psalm 22 (Mark 15:34); Luke substitutes "Father, into your hands I commend my spirit" (Luke 23:46). Some interpreters hold that Jesus actually had in mind the entire psalm, which ends on a positive note. But if the authors of Mark and Matthew had thought this, they would have said so; and if Luke had thought this as well, he would have at least alluded to the psalm's ending instead of reporting an entirely different saying.

alienate us from God either. In fact, Jesus' cry did not break his bond with God but rather expressed it, for he did not complain to those on the ground but asked his "Why?" directly to God. The Christian community praises the God of Jesus because only a God who accepts that cry is credible to those who suffer undeservedly—and yet not always credible to them[8]—for that cry has been taken into the heart of God.

In the last analysis, we do not know why the innocent suffer; what we do know is that this is part of the burden of our history, especially in the current century. But in light of Jesus we also believe that in the midst of suffering, when a Ms. Job urges the sufferer to curse God and die, true praise may be silence. The community of faith can acknowledge that even as it gathers to praise God. Praising God is the ultimate "Nevertheless!" It is the supreme act of faith.

Now that we have a sense of what praising God involves, we can see the extent to which the worship of God in mainline Protestantism has become secularized, and then how praising God can restore integrity to our worship and so be an antidote to that secularization itself. If in worship the church stands in the presence of God, then in praising God we meet the Creator—no small thing. Ernst Käsemann was right: "In the confrontation with the Creator, history ceases to be what we imagined it to be."[9]

Secularized Worship

If praise extols the excellence of another, and if praise is the heart of Christian worship, then worship is secularized

---

8. For example, a British chaplain in World War I, an Oswin Creighton, poured out his torment in a letter to his mother on Easter, 1918: "God so loved the world that he gave several millions of English begotten sons, that whosoever believeth in them should not perish, but have a comfortable life." Creighton too perished in the slaughter of that war. Quoted from David L. Edwards, *Christian England*, III, p. 360.

9. Ernst Käsemann, *The Testament of Jesus*, p. 34.

when the focus shifts from the character of God to the enhancement of ourselves, when *theocentrism* has been replaced by *anthropocentrism,* however much talk of God remains.[10] In fact, the secularized character of worship is manifest precisely in the ways God continues to be talked about, as well as in the ways God is hardly talked about at all.

Although the service usually retains much of the inherited vocabulary of worship, all too often the theocentric praise of God has been displaced by anthropocentric utilitarianism. What matters most is that everyone get something out of the service, as the phrase goes. So far as I can see, the feminist influence has been rather successful in minimizing the *androcentricity,* the male-centeredness, of worship, but it has by no means overcome the *anthropocentricity* of mainline worship. Instead, it may well have increased it by insisting that what is done and said enhance the agendas and the self-image of the worshiper. Where worship has been secularized, the worship of God is useful in helping us make actual our ideal secular selves: mature, self-motivated, able to develop our full potential, urbane in outlook, accepting and affirming of other people (especially those who insist on pursuing a different life-style), committed to social justice, concerned for body and earth, and above all feeling good about ourselves.

A sample service in a recent book shows how utilitarian worship can become. The call to confession "invites people to get in touch with themselves and asks where they feel some empty spaces in their lives" (symbolized by a display of empty, clear plastic bags on the communion table)—as if

---

10. Jay C. Rochelle asserts: "The aim of doxology is not to render ancient texts relevant to the person of today so much as it is to render each day relevant to the One who is lauded. . . . Doxology calls into consciousness an experienced reality by a name that has an identifiable historic meaning. The trinitarian name is thus the name of an experience, not a thing. When it becomes the name of a thing it has ceased to invoke reality" ("Doxology and the Trinity," in Braaten, in *Our Naming of God,* p. 131).

admitting emptiness were the same as confessing sin, and as if sin were merely the absence of good. Moreover, now the communion elements represent not Christ's passion but "our creative powers," which are transformed into expressions of Jesus Christ; now the breaking of the bread is not the point but the prelude to the point: "When we the committed loving people gather to let the pieces of Christ be reassembled in us" we have "our most powerful statement of wholism."[11] Such a Eucharist celebrates no longer the breaking of God's man that occurred for us but our potential for healing ourselves. This "most powerful statement of wholism" is nothing other than a modern example of Gnosticism.[12]

There are indeed positive, constructive, liberating, healing, and enlightening consequences of the worship of God. We do get perspective on ourselves and the world, and we do become motivated to address its wrongs. But the utilitarian mind gets the priorities wrong by making the by-product the main product. It forgets, and perhaps denies, that the worship of God is an end in itself.

If praise is the heart of worship, then making worship useful destroys it, because this introduces an ulterior motive for praise. And ulterior motives mean manipulation, taking charge of the relationship, thereby turning the relation between Creator and creature upside down. In this inversion, the living God, whose biblical qualities like jealousy and wrath have been tamed, has been deprived of freedom and, having been reduced to the Great Enabler, now has lit-

---

11. Thomas N. and Sharon N. Emswiler, *Wholeness in Worship*, p. 94. David R. Newman has seen what such worship actually means (*Worship as Praise and Empowerment*, p. 70).

12. Interestingly, the Canadian pastor, Philip J. Lee, finds Gnosticism throughout Protestantism today (*Against the Protestant Gnostics*). The initial chapter notes several features of Gnosticism: despair, alienation, ego-centered escape, and syncretism. The elastic nature of these categories allows him to find these traits throughout selected strands of Protestantism. Nonetheless, the book is frequently incisive.

tle to do except warrant our causes and help us fulfill our aspirations. This now completely benign deity may still evoke a sense of wonder, but little awe and less mystery, and no fear of the Lord at all. The opening line of the Westminster Confession is now reversed, for now the chief end of God is to glorify us and to be useful to us indefinitely.

It is little wonder that one can depart a mainline Protestant service that has become useful with the feeling that one has attended a public meeting or a rally with religious trappings. Such an experience, instead of being an alternative to the secularity that marks the world we live in and that lives in us, has become the Sunday morning instance of the same thing because here too the transcendence of God, the moral integrity of God vis-à-vis all human distortion of God, is in eclipse, while the remaining God-talk nurtures the illusion that there is no eclipse.[13] As a result, God has become an amiable bore, and worship a memorial service to a fire gone out.

Sadly, the secularization of Protestant worship is found not only in the mainline churches; it appears no less in those that regard themselves as "evangelical" or "charismatic." There too anthropocentrism reigns. Although the power of the transcendent God is indeed emphasized repeatedly, especially in healings, there too the utilitarian mind wants to manipulate it by urging us to pray harder.

Clearly secularized are many mainline Protestant funerals and memorial services. These ought to be occasions for celebrating forthrightly the Christian understanding of death

---

13. Everett C. Ladd claims that "religious commitments and scientific, rationalistic, secular views of the world exist side by side with little strain in most people in the United States" because they understand that the secular cannot deal with everything especially with what matters most ("Secular and Religious America," in Neuhaus, *Unsecular America,* p. 27). This positive explanation is not the only possible one. This lack of strain might also reflect the habit of partitioning life into zones, like Cyprus, so that going to church is like crossing from one zone to the other. Or the same absence of "strain" might reflect the secularization of religion itself.

and life as gifts from God. What we often get instead is a minimalist understatement of the Christian faith, coupled with an exaggerated encomium for the dead. The event is shaped according to the desires of the customers, even if no fee is paid. Apart from Scripture readings and a brief prayer, all too often the whole thing is a secular event, the content and spirit of which celebrate more the alleged virtues of the departed than those of the Living One whom the invocation invited but who was then marginalized by the service itself.

Secularization is virtually complete in many Protestant weddings. Usually the focus of attention is on the bride; everyone else is an ornament, including the mothers. The ritual itself is all too often restructured according to whims of the customers. Even the clergy have become ornaments, as when a woman called the dean's office to make arrangements for her daughter's wedding here in the Divinity School's Marquand Chapel. Not only did she need an ordained minister as well as a chapel, but she wanted a Presbyterian who was young and handsome—one who would look nice in the pictures. Another wanted a center aisle for her daughter's procession so fervently that she offered to replace all the pews. The churches would be better off if they ceased functioning as agents of the state and got out of the marrying business altogether, and if, like their European counterparts, they blessed and celebrated in worship the marriages that had occurred legally before a civil magistrate.

If there be any remaining doubt about the secularization of much mainline worship, one need only study what has happened to the church year—the institutionalized embodiment of the churches' self-understanding. Having become program-dominated, the churches find it inevitable that their year really begins after Labor Day, when vacations are over for those families whose children return to school. Thereby the classical beginning of the church year on

Advent Sunday is quietly down-graded to another "special Sunday."

More significant is the fact that apart from those Sundays that are unavoidably governed by the Christian faith (Christmas, Easter, Pentecost), the remaining Sundays have become public relations events for programs, activities, and emphases—except for the summer months when some churches' programs go into hibernation anyway. One denominational calendar identifies fourteen of the remaining thirty-one Sundays as promotional days, sometimes listing two emphases for the same Sunday. A congregation following such a calendar—probably rare, fortunately—would soon find the worship and the praise of God reduced to a formality, not unlike the "opening exercises" in the old-time Sunday School. Such Sundays are "useful" for promoting the agendas of denominational bureaucrats and special interest groups within the churches; nonetheless, all too often on such Sundays what remains of the worship portion of the hour is related to the real, vital worship of God as junk food is related to a banquet.

Praise and Renewal

According to David Newman, praise is "an action that has no other purpose but to glorify the Giver of life, and is, therefore, purposeless as regards our human plans and programs. It is the ultimate metaphor of discontinuity. . . . Praise is empowerment because it does not intend to be."[14] And he is on target. So pervasive has become the anthropocentrism of worship that unless purposeless praise of God is restored to its central place in worship, mainline Protestantism will not be renewed. Only purposeless praise can cope effectively with our narcissism, with the grossness of

---

14. *Worship as Praise and Empowerment*, pp. 103-4.

our self-preoccupation even in worshiping the Creator, because by definition praise is not a means to an end but the end itself. If the transcendent God-Reality is indeed praiseworthy, then it is to be praised for what it is and not for what our fulsome talk will get it to do for us. Indeed, if the gospel is reliable, God is to be praised because of what has already been done for us, and will be done for us, that we cannot do for ourselves, because that is the kind of Reality God is. In praising God we know that this Reality has power sufficient to save us from the folly of our wisdom and from the weakness of our power.

If that be the case, let me paraphrase the Apostle again: How will people praise God if they have not believed? And how are they to believe in God if they have not heard who God really is? And how are they to hear if the preacher does not make it clear? (Rom. 10:14-15). In other words, in the praiseful worship of God, the role of preaching is vital. In fact, renewal, preaching, and praise belong together.

That preaching has taken on many tasks is all too clear. Not so clear is why facilitating the praise of God is rarely one of them. Yes, expounding the greatness and goodness of God, the transcendence and freedom of God to be God, is not easy in a time when any talk of God is either difficult or glib. Yes, we want our preaching to be helpful and germane to the lives of those who listen. But is it not helpful and germane to put the disarray of life into the perspective of God's greatness, of God's judgment and mercy? Unfortunately, one can attend many mainline Protestant churches every Sunday for years and seldom hear the greatness, the judgment and mercy, freedom and integrity of God brought to bear on the day-to-day. Allusion to God has replaced affirmation and proclamation. Even in the churches that use the Apostles' Creed the sermons rarely expound what is confessed. True, the sermon is not a lecture. But better to be instructed in the Creed than to be given common sense about better living or the clergy's exasperations with United States foreign policy—things gotten more easily, and probably more interestingly, from the op-ed page of the Sunday paper. In any case, it belongs to the preaching task to sort out the truth of God from the illusions of God, and to make the truth of God explicit. Where the truth of God is veiled in vagueness, there will be no praise but only a positive attitude toward the Ultimate.

Since the renewal of the mainline churches requires a reform of their secularized worship, which in turn entails restoring its focus on the purposeless praise of God, we cannot avoid asking, What renews the praise of God? The answer too is unavoidable: a fresh apprehension of the truth of God. How that apprehension is to come about, on the other hand, is not prescribable, though what occurs when it comes about is describable. For example, for some it will be primarily an experience of God's grace, while for others it will be primarily a fresh understanding of the grace already experienced. For others it will be the discovery, whether painful or ecstatic, of the difference between believing one's beliefs about God and believing in God. In light of what was observed about the nature of praise at the beginning of this chapter, praise of God is renewed when some aspect of God's character comes through so convincingly that it must be acknowledged gratefully. The truth of God that renews praise is experienced truth, life's validating Yes to the gospel, whether taught, preached, sung, or enacted.

Finally, because praise is the joyful celebration of the excellence of another, there is no such thing as joyless praise of God. Where the news of God is clear and good, it evokes joy in those who receive it. In fact, one may well ask whether the gospel has been believed if our feet are not freed to dance and our tongues to sing.[15] I cannot avoid the suspicion that one reason that neoorthodoxy did not really renew the

---

15. The role of bodily movement in worship is noted often. *See,* e.g., Marianne H. Micks, *The Future Present,* chap. 2.

mainline churches is that, however much it sobered their theology, it gave them no song to sing and produced no hymnody of note. Be that as it may, the experience of the Protestant Reformation, the Wesleyan movement, the revivals on the American frontier, and the Catholic Church today, shows that when the greatness of God becomes real, the church is renewed, and there is joy in the heart and a song on the lips of the people of God. All too often, however, the present situation is epitomized by a memorable scene: Adjacent to a church was a restaurant whose kitchen equipment evidently needed attention. Parked beside the church was the mechanics' truck whose sign may well have been appropriate for both the restaurant and the church: "Refrigerated Services."

I do not know why so much of mainline Protestantism has become a joyless religion. Perhaps we are more impressed by the problems of the world than by the power of God. Perhaps we have become so secular that we indeed think that now everything depends on us; that surely ought to make us depressed. Perhaps we have simply gotten bored with a boring God whom we substituted for the God of the Bible. We sometimes sing the Doxology as if it were a dirge. Even the Eucharist, despite the words of the Great Thanksgiving, is rarely the thankful, joyous foretaste of the Great Banquet with the One who triumphed over Death,[16] but mostly a mournful occasion for introspection. A joyless Christianity is as clear a sign that something is amiss as a dirty church.

If the predominantly white mainliners can learn anything from their black brothers and sisters, it is the power of joyful

---

16. Geoffrey Wainwright observes that in the Western liturgical tradition, "the Eucharist prayer constitutes for the believing community a *climax of praise, toward which* the liturgical sequence of Scripture lessons, sermons and creed has been leading" ("The Praise of God in the Theological Reflection of the Church," p. 39, italics added). If this rationale were allowed to shape what happens on "Communion Sunday," would it not transform the "observance" of the Lord's Supper into a "celebration"?

praise in the face of deprivation, prejudice, and suffering. They dare to celebrate the great *Nevertheless* because they know that despite everything, God is God. And in that joyous praise they find power to endure and to change the world.

To be sure, there have been many attempts to make the worship of God more joyous. On the one hand, we have deleted the somber aspects of God, thereby ignoring the tart warning by that relentless opponent of liberal theology, J. Gresham Machen, that "religion cannot be made joyful simply by looking on the bright side of God."[17] On the other hand, we have blown up balloons, danced in the aisles, marched behind banners; we have turned to jazz and we have sung ditties whose theological content makes a nursery rhyme sound like Thomas Aquinas. But it is not enough to make things livelier, or set to music our aspirations and agendas. We can do better than that, and we must, for when the truth of God as made actual in Christ and attested in the gospel evokes the truthful praise of God, Christian worship enacts an alternative to the secularism which otherwise deludes us with its promises.

Now if the praise of God is the right response to the truth of God, then the renewal of the mainline churches requires also that they get serious about theology. In fact, praising God might even renew theology—if theology attends carefully to what Christians mean and do not mean when they praise God (as well as pray or complain to God), and to what happens to their modes of thinking and living as a result.[18] The state of current theology, and its possible renewal, is therefore the theme of the next chapter.

---

17. J. Gresham Machen, *Christianity and Liberalism*, p. 134.

18. Renewing theology is much less a matter of making theological discourse *possible* by appealing for legitimation to some extraneous, allegedly neutral conceptuality or epistemology than is often assumed. This is why Paul L. Holmer denies that metaphysics "somehow bestows meaning on more ordinary expression" and contends that we give meaning to language, not by thinking abstract correlatives (e.g., "Ground of Being" instead of "God") but rather by "putting the language to work as hard and as thoroughly as possible" (*The Grammar of Faith*, pp. 129, 128).

CHAPTER TWO

THEOLOGY

Theology, if it is to be of real use to the preacher, must be modernized . . . if theology is to be modernized it must be by its own gospel.

—P. T. Forsyth, *Positive Preaching and the Modern Mind*

Many avant-garde theologians regard the current interest in revelation to be the terminal gasp of a dying mainstream Christian culture as it struggles to reassert its hegemony in a world splintered by theologies of this or theologies of that.

—Mark Wallace, *The Second Naivete*

For us Tradition is on the way to becoming something we know about but do not live.

—Robert N. Bellah, *The Broken Covenant*

An undogmatic faith is, at the very least, a decision against the Fourth Gospel.

—Ernst Käsemann, *The Testament of Jesus*

T he foregoing chapter claimed that if the so-called mainline churches are to be renewed, their worship of God must recover its focus on the praise of God. Making central the praise of God requires that the truth of God and of ourselves be understood well, affirmed boldly, and taught affirmatively. Otherwise, praise becomes a perfunctory exercise in flattery whose consequences for the churches are serious: They will dissipate their identities and have less and less to transmit to the next generation.

This truth about God and ourselves is not an invention of today's church, but is first of all a patrimony from our predecessors, and only secondarily the result of current efforts to state it afresh, necessary as they are. In other words, the church's understanding of the faith must be achieved again and again. Otherwise, we will confuse what Jaroslav Pelikan's epigram distinguished—namely, the living faith of the dead and the dead faith of the living.[1]

Consequently, this chapter turns to the renewal of serious theology in the mainline churches. These churches, despite their ample theological heritage, are no longer seriously teaching the theological substance of the Christian faith. Repeatedly they have abandoned opportunities to ground people more deeply in the faith. Their Sunday worship services have forfeited their educative role. Often the children are excused early, taking their teachers with them—as if the worship service were an R-rated event. But even if they remain, the teaching of the Christian faith in the Sunday morning service is minimal. And in most mainline congregations, only the elderly can recall going to church on Sunday night. Even the pastor's best opportunity to teach the faith to the rising generation—confirmation—

---

1. "Tradition is the living faith of the dead; traditionalism is the dead faith of the living," Jaroslav Pelikan, *The Vindication of Tradition,* p. 65.

appears to be more dreaded than welcomed. Indeed, a recently popular book transforms confirmation as instruction in the faith into a rite of passage into Christian adulthood.[2] Nonetheless, the mainline churches have inherited theological wealth sufficient to serve substantial theological fare, but all too often they offer little more than potato skins to those who hunger for a real meal. Indeed, the churches are suffering from theological anorexia themselves.

One factor in the situation is the legacy of the bitter, and often futile, arguments with fundamentalism, which tore congregations, denominations, and seminaries apart, and alienated colleagues. Understandably, we prefer polite silence to controversy. More important, Protestantism's congenital inability to value and incorporate dissent has in recent years been legitimated by the mainliners' resolve to be open, inclusive, loving, affirming communities, implying that all opinions—from the bizarre to the banal—are welcome so long as they do not challenge the institution itself. If those who disagree do not want to be disagreeable, they remain silent, so that there are often a few loud talkers and many docile hearers, not believing what they hear but not wanting to ostracize themselves by creating a stir. Inevitably, there emerges an outlook according to which the church survives better, indeed thrives, without attending to theological issues at all. They simply do not matter anymore because people are being helped and find church meaningful without them. Probably the most important factor in the situation is the manifest uncertainty about the substance of the Christian faith itself. This uncertainty reflects what has happened to theology in recent years. And since our theme is renewal and reform and not

---

2. William O. Roberts, Jr., *Initiation to Adulthood: An Ancient Rite of Passage in Contemporary Form* (New York: Pilgrim Press, 1983).

improvement, the following review of the theological scene is largely critical.

Four Shifts in Theology

Today, theology—broadly understood—is like a state fair without a midway: Everything is going on at the same time and there is no main exhibit. The 1991 spring issue of *Books and Religion* reported the best-sellers in five bookstores that serve primarily seminaries in five cities. No two stores reported the same book as number 1, 2, or 3, and of fifty books, only three appeared on three lists and not one of the fifty was an important work in theology. In part, this reflects the arrival of new exhibitors at the fair—women, minorities, and the voices of the former Third World. I suspect that before long we shall see also new exhibits from Eastern Europe and the former Soviet Union, whose hearty borscht and goulash will show just how thin has been the theological soup served by American mainliners. In any case, the new exhibitors have not simply added their own booths but frequently have challenged the fair itself.

My intent here, however, is not to conduct a tour of the fair where each exhibit clamors for attention and claims to be the way to the future. The aim, rather, is to characterize the scene as a whole. Consequently, I am not describing any particular place or attributing to all exhibitors what is true of a few. It is the overall picture that is important, and it reflects four important shifts.

Theology Becomes Anthropology

To begin with, much North American theology has virtually become anthropology because it is convinced that the nature of language requires us to be agnostic about God. That is, there is no way of knowing whether our language about God really describes the Reality of which it speaks because no one can test its accuracy. The late bishop J. A. T. Robinson went even farther: "As soon as we pass beyond the limited area verifiable in the experience of our relationship with other people and things, there is *nothing* to count for or against the truth of our assertions."[3] The triumph of empiricism could hardly be stated more clearly. But this is by no means the end of the matter, for the bishop evidently dismissed two criteria for truth—coherence and consequences. The latter criterion has become especially important, as we shall see. But first, the agnosticism of theology as well as the turn to anthropology requires brief comment.[4]

That the language of theology is unavoidably agnostic is hardly a new idea, though tracing it through the medieval controversies between the realists and the nominalists to its roots requires more competence than I have. It suffices to remember that two centuries ago Immanuel Kant undermined the arguments for the existence of God by showing that our language is derived from the phenomenal world and therefore cannot be applied to the nonphenomenal, the noumenal realm whose existence we may posit but cannot demonstrate.[5] Metaphysics has been on the defensive ever since (process theology being an exception).[6] Current deconstructionist thought goes even farther, contending that language doesn't

---

3. John A. T. Robinson, *The New Reformation?* pp. 23-24 (italics added).

4. Rudolf Bultmann was a leading forerunner in the conversion of theology into anthropology, for he insisted that one must not speak of God as an object of knowledge like other objects; however, since the understanding of God and *Mensch* ("man," not male) are correlates, analysis of the structures of human existence in our self-understanding points to God. For Bultmann, insisting on the non-objectifiability of God protects divine transcendence.

5. Kant's contention is axiomatic for the work of Gordon D. Kaufman. *See*, e.g., Kaufman's brief but lucid exposition of Kant in "Metaphysics and Theology," in *The Theological Imagination,* pp. 242-44.

6. Charles Peirce, a founder of pragmatism, spoke for many: "Metaphysics is a subject much more curious than useful, the knowledge of which, like that of a sunken reef, serves chiefly to enable us to keep clear of it." Quoted from William A. Dyrness, *How Does America Hear the Gospel?* p. 44.

necessarily refer to anything at all beyond itself. Even apart from that extreme view, Kant's point no longer startles, and it would be hard to find a theologian anywhere who claimed that any human language, rooted in the phenomenal world we know, can describe accurately that nonphenomenal Reality we call God. If empirical verifiability is the criterion of our language about God, we must indeed be agnostic, for we do not and cannot know that God-Reality so directly that we can assess the adequacy of our language to speak of it.

But I see no reason to bewail that it is so. To the contrary, Christian theology must insist that the God-Reality with which it is concerned is not an empirically demonstrable deity. A demonstrable god is a curiosity but not the Creator. Moreover, if one could show that the God-Reality of which we speak corresponds precisely to our language, our relation to it would be no longer one of faith but one of knowledge, and we would become Gnostics. To be sure, faith is not believing what we know isn't so; but it is trusting beyond the demonstrable. It entails believing that our language can speak authentically, though not with descriptive accuracy, about God even if it must at times rely on the *via negativa*, like "immortal" and "invisible," to say what God is not. Although we have known this for centuries, what is being said in some quarters today goes much farther.

Sometimes brief books designed for the general reader reveal the unfortunate situation better than large, subtle, technical tomes with their in-house debates and jargon.[7] So it is, I believe, with Daniel Liechty's 100-page *Theology in Postliberal Perspective*,[8] which, having taken deconstruction

---

7. A convenient overview of recent and current discussions of "the God problem" is provided by Carl E. Braaten, "The Problem of God-Language Today," in *Our Naming of God*, chap. 1 (esp. "On the Referentiality of God-language," pp. 23-26).

8. Daniel Liechty, *Theology in Postliberal Perspective* (Philadelphia: Trinity Press International; London: SCM Press, 1990). Page numbers in parentheses refer to this work.

seriously,[9] attempts to make a case for the continuing legitimacy of theology nonetheless. He declares flatly that "the idea of God is surely wish fulfillment" and that while "sometimes human desires and hopes correspond to reality . . . our reason can only leave us with an open question" about the actual existence of God. Clearly, the God who may exist may as well not exist, because that Reality does not disclose its existence. But it would not matter if God did so, for we cannot get beyond our images, constructs, and models for God—and apparently neither can God!

According to Liechty, "A particular construct or model for God is not 'true' because it accurately describes an object to which it corresponds." Rather, its truth is determined by the degree to which it supports "creative, transcending and loving works." Because God-talk has this function, "God becomes our responsibility," as he puts it. Indeed, "The only God who can save us from our predicament is the God whom we construct. . . . We alone may construct this image of God [i.e., one which saves by promoting our well-being]. This God is, therefore, fully incarnate in human history" (pp. 33-37)—a rather banal assertion, since this God is extrapolated from ourselves.

Although this approach cannot distinguish the real God from imitations and substitutes, Liechty insists that religious experiences are real (p. 185); but who can deny that adoring our own creation can be a real experience? When he says

---

9. As a revolt against the whole assumption that language refers to anything other than language, "the movement of deconstruction has set about to show that the cathedral of modern intellect is but a mirage in a cloud—cuckooland," as Carl Raschke puts it. This means that theology's task is *"the composition of epitaphs."* Deconstruction—"the interior drive of twentieth century theology rather than an alien agenda"—is nothing more than *"the death of God put into writing"* ("The Deconstruction of God," in T. J. J. Altizer, et al., eds., *Deconstruction and Theology,* pp. 3-4, italics in original). The oracular and apodictic character of this essay is virtually a parody of Moses: Like the biblical figure, who confronted Golden-calf worshipers, Raschke, bearing the revelation from Derrida and Foucault delivered on a French Sinai, thunders at those who think language can refer to what is real.

that "Christian theology begins with the experience of God as love" (p. 98), he must mean that our self-constructed "God" loves us. The poor thing could hardly do otherwise.

The Kantian contention has been reinforced by the sociology of knowledge, which has claimed that the socioeconomic status of the knower affects what is known and how it is known. Consequently, theology began to insist that only those images and models for God are allowable which support the goals of social justice. All others are to be rejected because they have been linked with patterns of domination. Feminist theology has been especially adamant in this regard. However, it is one thing to affirm the goal of real equality of women and men, especially in the church (as I do), another to tie that so tightly to our language that the Reality we call "God" is deprived of its own integrity and freedom to be itself. For example, Marjorie Procter-Smith's vigorously argued book on liturgy faults both gender neutral and inclusive language for not going far enough; only emancipatory language will do— language which explicitly relies on female imagery, including God's female body.[10] Like many others, she writes under enormous pressure to find only flawless language about God. Yet nowhere does she raise the' question of the truth of God itself, despite repeated references to "the living God." Nor, if a pun is permitted, is it ever clear what this God does for a living.

Fortunately, Sallie McFague's book, *Metaphorical Theology*, is wiser, partly because she is alert to the limitations of any image, model, or metaphor, and partly because she recognizes the need for several kinds of language, including the impersonal.[11] Above all, she explicitly raises the issue of the

---

10. Marjorie Procter-Smith, *In Her Own Rite: Constructing Feminist Liturgical Tradition*.

11. She points out that even God as "friend" needs to be supplemented by "models which differentiate between the status of friends"—those which suggest "guidance, leadership, protection, governance and preeminence"; so too we need more impersonal language "that expresses experiences of awe, ecstasy, fear and silence in relation to God" (*Metaphorical Theology*, p. 191).

truthfulness of all models (pp. 131-37), lest they become only "desperate attempts to say *something* when we do not know what else to say" (p. 131). She asserts that metaphors and models "*do* refer to reality, but as redescriptions of it," which are inherently in tension with that reality (p. 136). And that is the key point. In other words, our language—our images, metaphors, and models—permits us to say something that is valid though incomplete and inadequate, and the user does not need to be told so by an empiricist but knows it precisely when using it. Which is why powerful religious language creates dramatic, language-bending metaphors.

This is what Janet Martin Soskice has seen. Her astute book *Metaphor and Religious Language* defends a critical realism that claims "to speak of God without claiming to define him, and to do so by means of metaphor," and argues that our language about God is "referential without being tied to unreviseable description" (p. 148). Our metaphoric language about God, she points out, "denominates rather than describes God"—that is, it names and characterizes what we are talking about (p. 154; made more precise by the rest of the sentence). At the same time our language filters and distorts it.[12] This is precisely how our finitude and fallibility, our creaturehood and our historicity, affect our thinking and speaking of God, for which we *are* responsible—as Gordon Kaufman has reminded us repeatedly. Fortunately, the grosser distortions can be corrected. The recent insistence on using non-gender-specific language for God has freed many of us from unwitting distortions in our thinking of God, and for that we are grateful.

What is truly pivotal, however, is whether that God-Reality also communicates itself through our fragile thinking and speaking, and whether in doing so it also alerts us (and not only the savants

---

12. Soskice points out that any realist position inherently must allow for the possibility of error.

of language) to our distortions.[13] In short, can we still affirm divine self-revelation through the limits of our language, or is God even more frustrated by it than we are? The game is over if this Reality is not free to disclose itself through our language while at the same time breaking it sufficiently to inhibit our absolutizing it. A deity that is inert and incompetent is no deity at all.

But other things must be said as well. For one thing, correlating speech and social status is a game that everyone can play with everyone else; the correlation applies as much to the advocates of new language as to the users of the old, because even if a flawless language for God could be invented—one that is not guilty of begetting or abetting some social sin—only sinners with a specific social location would use it, and so misuse that also. Or are we to think that using flawless language makes users flawless?

Lurking behind the demand for flawless words is a technological view of language—that is, the passion to understand how language works is driven by the desire to control its use, to manipulate it for desired goals. This is surely the mindset of the secularized opinion-makers, the new class to which Peter Berger has called attention.[14] What makes this

13. It is precisely at this point that I find a lack of clarity in Kaufman's work (from which I have learned much). While insisting that *we* construct our concepts of God, he also asserts "that it is precisely through the constructive work of the human imagination that God . . . makes himself known." Gordon D. Kaufman, *An Essay on Theological Method,* pp. 67-68. Moreover, even if "God" functions as "the ultimate point of reference," it is still we who do the referencing. It is not clear whether this Ultimate Reference Point is more than a logical inference.

14. Berger speaks of "a burgeoning 'new class' of intellectuals deeply antagonistic to virtually all the old norms of respectability. It is consumption-oriented rather than production-oriented. Its values for private life are ever more radically liberationist. It is pervasively secularized, often evincing a violent antipathy to all traditional forms of Christian and Jewish religiosity . . . the intellectuals suffer increasingly from a profound sense of homelessness," *Facing Up to Modernity,* p. 66. More recently Berger called attention to the link between this "new class" and the "knowledge industry," and also noted that because it is a "*rising* class" it is in conflict with the older, established middle class. He also observed that while the mainline churches still contain a (dwindling) number of the latter, the clergy have identified almost completely with the former. "Different Gospels: The Social Sources of Apostasy," in Neuhaus, *American Apostasy,* pp. 4-5.

technological view of language so attractive during the eclipse of God and the entropy of religious vitality in the mainline churches is the implication that proper (i.e., "politically correct") manipulation of metaphors can bring God back and vivify proper religious experience. Indeed, wherever the God-Reality has been collapsed into our language for God, one can scarcely avoid thinking that changing God-language changes God too, making us the creators and shapers of God instead of acknowledging that it is we who are the created and the shaped.

Finally, despite the concern to transform the conditions of our earthbound existence, when theology becomes preoccupied with the language-society correlation, it easily becomes Gnostic in its character, and supralapsarian (before "the Fall") in content. It becomes *Gnostic* because, with respect to our relation to God, the central categories are not moral but conceptual, noetic, and linguistic. It becomes *supralapsarian* because, by insisting that only untainted language about God is valid, it accepts only language unaffected by the Fall—if such can be invented. And why not use only untainted language if "God" is being constructed according to specifications derived directly from our social goals?

Gospel Becomes Law

Because much current theology has tacitly replaced gospel with law, it offers little basis for Good News, except perhaps for the alleged beneficiaries of current "class action" theology. The classical Christian understanding of the gospel— the Good News that in Christ God has done for us what we could not do for ourselves—has been replaced by the announcement that because the destiny of the world is in our hands only, we must work harder than ever to save it. Sometimes it is implied that it is wrong to expect God to do it. But for whom is this news good? Mostly for the rising middle class, which no longer needs to direct its energies toward securing a good life for itself and feels guilty for having inherited it. The issue of course is much deeper, for it pivots on the significance of the Christ-event for the human condition. The history of Christology shows that the significance of Jesus is regularly construed in ways that fit the understanding of the human condition and its remedy. Thus, if the heart of the human dilemma is ignorance, the saving remedy is knowledge, and Christ is the Teacher. The more profound the ignorance, the more exalted the Person and Work of Christ must be to deal with it decisively. Given this correlation between Christology and soteriology (the doctrine of salvation), it is quite understandable that any "do it yourself" theology has no real place for the atonement, for atonement implies that a perverted relation to God lies at the heart of the human condition, as the New Testament asserts. Atonement is no longer necessary when sin has been displaced by ignorance as the root of the problem or when sin has been made manageable by being viewed as transgression, and its cumulative, systemic result not seen as a condition so insidious that we cannot free ourselves from it.

Admittedly, the atonement is not the sole meaning of Jesus for the human condition, but considering it alerts us to what becomes of Jesus' execution when this doctrine is abandoned. In a word, then Jesus' death tells us about his commitment to God's kingdom, but nothing about God's commitment of the kingdom to us that we did not know before. Then Jesus' death was a hero's death even though it was not as heroic as that of Socrates or even of Jesus' followers, some of whom gladly met their executioners. Without the atonement, Jesus' death also shows us what happens to a good man when entrenched power perceives him to be a threat. In one way or another, depending on what one regards as constitutive of Jesus' mission, the death becomes an illustration, perhaps even an inspiring one. But by definition, an illustration is not a revelation; it is a vivid instance of what we knew already.[15] It discloses nothing new or decisive about God, the world, sin, goodness, or power. Jesus' death might disclose unforgettably the depth of human sinfulness, but unless that death is somehow God's deed on our behalf, simply understanding sin better gives us a clearer diagnosis but no healing. And this is precisely where the currently popular portrayal of Jesus as a leader of a reform movement leaves us—with a pre-Christian understanding of salvation as our obligatory project in the face of enormous odds.[16]

This critique does not repudiate the need to achieve a more just and humane society, or to do what we can to heal the earth we have ravaged, and to do so as disciples of Jesus. The point, rather, is that seeing Jesus essentially as a martyr not only turns Jesus the gift into an obligation but also limits his meaning to those aspects of the human plight that can be addressed adequately by our own activity. The deeper dilemmas of the self, whether seen with the eyes of Paul or of John, for instance, are bypassed and sometimes disdained as diversionary for the sake of a this-worldly salvation by works that are appropriate for secularized middle-class achievers. But where is the Good News for the self that fails, that faces meaninglessness, despair, futility, as well as the tyranny of disease and Death? Can reconciliation with God really be found by involvement in good causes? Do we receive God's forgiveness because we repent—because we change our ways—or do we repent because we have accepted God's forgiveness? In short, far too much theology today underwrites a striver's manual instead of a gift certificate from the God who, in Paul's words, justifies the ungodly (Rom. 4:5).

---

15. Robert W. Jensen's comment regarding Christology is to the point: "Christological propositions are right insofar as they compendiously and drastically *offend* any culture's and any generation's self-evidence about God." "A 'Protestant Constructive Response' to Christian Unbelief," in Neuhaus, *American Apostasy*, p. 64.

16. Thomas C. Oden, *After Modernity . . . What?* p. 131.

Now Understanding Seeks Faith

Much theology has reversed Anselm's famous insight that theology is faith seeking understanding. Nine centuries ago, Anselm of Canterbury insisted that the task of theology is not to make it possible to believe the Christian faith but to understand the faith one already has. Insofar as today's theology is propelled and controlled by prior commitments to an agenda for social change, this relation of faith and knowledge is reversed. Now the question is whether, and perhaps to what extent, the Christian faith is yet compatible with and supportive of those commitments, grounded in a theory and its method of analyzing and explaining human life in society. Instead of ascertaining what resources are available for illuminating the faith, now the task is to ascertain what the faith might contribute to a nonnegotiable agenda which is both logically prior to and politically more urgent than the faith itself. Instead of asking, Given my allegiance to the gospel and to the theological structure that supports it, what should my commitments be? current theology asks, Given my commitments, can I still believe the gospel and avow the theology that goes with it? Instead of finding in the Christian tradition a way of reading the world, this reversal of Anselm leads today's theology to find in the world a way of reading the Christian tradition in the hope that faith of some sort is yet possible. We recall Hans Frei's observation that whereas the Bible once provided the lens through which reality was made intelligible, now a view of reality is the lens through which the Bible is read, and I might add, assessed and often found wanting.[17]

The classic liberal Protestant theologies addressed the intellectual difficulties in the received tradition—things like the three-story universe, miracles, or a literal Second Coming—

---

17. Hans W. Frei, *The Eclipse of Biblical Narrative: A Study in Enlightenment and Nineteenth-century Hermeneutics* (New York and London: Yale University Press, 1974).

but the current objections to Christianity present themselves as moral. Much of today's theology struggles with the substance of Christianity itself lest affirming it be an immoral act. Indeed, Patricia Wilson-Kastner observes, "To refer to 'God' in certain feminist circles is sometimes perceived as a hostile act, or at best one emerging from ignorance."[18] It is not particular beliefs that are objectionable (as in Bishop Robinson's *But That I Can't Believe*) but the faith itself because the culture it shaped is being condemned wholesale. That non-Christians find the Christian faith objectionable is not new, for already the apostle Paul wrote about the *skandalon* of the cross. What is new is that the antipathy toward the Christian tradition and its culture now comes from Christian theologians themselves. As a result, the polemical edge of their theology is aimed not at the assumptions and assertions deemed contrary to Christian faith but against the Christian heritage itself. What was once refuted can now be celebrated as wrongly suppressed truth. Not surprisingly, Gnosticism, polytheism, and syncretism have been affirmed; Manichaeism too has revived, for when this theology is criticized its advocates view themselves as righteous victims in a world controlled by reactionary connivers against righteousness and truth.

This turnabout does not characterize the whole theological scene, of course. The situation is comparable to that of the late sixties, when the impression was abroad that American youth were in wholesale rebellion, whereas the majority continued to be rather traditional. Indeed, there are signs that in many quarters the classical Christian theological tradition is again being studied and taught more seriously.[19]

---

18. *Faith, Feminism, and the Christ,* p. 20.

19. In 1991, Gabriel Fackre's presidential address to the American Theological Society presented the results of a survey of the teaching of theology, which substantiate this observation. The published version of Fackre's address, "Reorientation and Retrieval in Systematic Theology," appeared in *The Christian Century* 108, no. 20 (June 26–July 3, 1991): 653-56.

Nonetheless, the changes in theology have been influential, even among the more tradition-minded, because they tapped into a powerful emotion, silently waiting to be energized—namely, a deep alienation.

The Hermeneutic of Suspicion Becomes the Hermeneutic of Alienation

The fourth aspect of the current theological scene is now in view—the *hermeneutic of suspicion* has become the *hermeneutic of alienation.* This alienation has become both the unquestioned starting point and the guiding principle for reading reality; it is not simply one factor among others but a hermeneutic. What shifting to a hermeneutic of alienation means will be clearer if we first recall the nature and purpose of the hermeneutic of suspicion.

The hermeneutic of suspicion has been fundamental in modern historiography and so has come to govern the historical-critical study of the Bible and of the formation of Christian doctrine as well. In fact, it has become axiomatic for all inquiry that distinguishes, as a matter of principle, what we are told from the truth of the matter. The hermeneutic of suspicion puts the burden of proof on the evidence by requiring it to substantiate its credibility as strongly as possible. After Freud every pastoral counselor distinguishes the reasons people give from the real reasons. The hermeneutic of suspicion has become as essential for the modern intellectual as for the investigative reporter: Both withhold credence as a matter of principle until the reliability of information has been assessed.

But the hermeneutic of alienation goes farther. Whereas the hermeneutic of suspicion interrogates evidence in order to find the truth, the hermeneutic of alienation interrogates it in order to document an alleged truth already in hand. In the hermeneutic of suspicion the tradition is tested in order to establish its degree of credibility to an unprejudiced observer, but in the hermeneutic of alienation the tradition is accused so that the committed righteous can distance themselves from it.

The motor that drives this hermeneutic of alienation is moral outrage at the world's evils, on the one hand, and the need to deal with a sense of guilt for participating in them and benefiting from them, on the other. Christian moral outrage is not new, but it is doubtful whether ever before it has been so potent a factor in theology, for it has persuaded many that the truthfulness of Christian theology must be judged in political terms first of all. Much modern theology has adapted what Karl Marx asserted about philosophy: Up to now philosophers have attempted to understand the world; the task, however, is to change it. No more will religion be accused of being the opium of the people; now it will be the elixir of revolution, for now salvation pertains first of all to the redistribution of earthly goods and power. For centuries the central question of theology, as of all thought, was, Is it true?; in many quarters today, the paramount question is now, Who benefits?[20] That this is a legitimate question is obvious. What is by no means obvious is how it is to be answered or what span of time is to be considered—though the alienated who have handed out only white and black hats always know. What Lewis Feuer observed in another context is true also of the ideology-industrial complex which supplies theological weapons for the class war, namely: Ideas are evaluated primarily for their firepower.[21]

---

20. How different today's mindset is from that of thirty-five years ago is revealed by the opening sentence of Reinhold Niebuhr's essay, "Liberty and Equality" (first published in 1957): "Insofar as the debate between conservatism and liberalism is a contest between the beneficiaries and the victims of any given status quo, it may be politically potent but it is philosophically uninteresting. It merely reveals the ideological taint in our political preference" (*Pious and Secular America*, p. 61). Much of today's theology would insist on reversing this view.

21. Lewis S. Feuer, *Ideology and the Ideologists*, p. 190. This perceptive study is illuminative also of modern theology, not Feuer's concern.

There are indeed plenty of situations in the world that rightly evoke moral outrage. And not a word of my criticism of alienated theology implies justification of oppression, torture, abject poverty, and relentless hunger, which many fellow humans endure. Nor can it be denied that religions, including the Christian one, have acquiesced in this dreadful story, the underbelly of history. The point, however, is that if Christian theology is going to make moral outrage the motor of theological reconstruction, it ought to do so in the name of Romans 1:18, according to which God's wrath is revealed from heaven against *all* human wickedness, wherever it is found, because everybody's last name is Adam.

Understandably, alienation is an appealing way of dealing with one's complicity in situations that evoke moral outrage, for it puts one on the side of the angels. Distancing oneself from wicked institutions and their malign "false consciousness" also reinforces one's own rectitude. With alienation goes the need to identify and to identify with those who are either at the edge or on the bottom of the established system, for such self-identification atones for the guilt of complicity. But Karl Marx, who developed the idea of alienation in the first place, showed that one does not actually need to live in solidarity with the oppressed, for he never once visited a factory or associated with poor workers. It was all in his head, and cost him nothing.[22] A nineteenth-century imperialist missionary living in a compound had more solidarity with the "heathen" than Marx had with the poor workers by writing secular apocalyptic in the British Museum.

Four consequences of alienation-driven theology deserve mention. First, almost any idea gains credence today if its advocates claim to be motivated by identification with the poor, the powerless, and the oppressed. Even the long-discredited legend that Jesus was the illegitimate offspring of

---

22. Paul Johnson, *Intellectuals*, chap. 3.

a vulnerable Jewish girl who during her betrothal was seduced or raped, perhaps by a Roman officer (whom the Nazis identified as an Aryan), has been rehabilitated because it is said to show God's concern for the marginalized and the subversion of patriarchy.[23]

Second, a theology with such warrants adds to the burden of proof the burden of guilt. When one participant in theological discourse claims the high moral ground and so tacitly accuses the critical partner of supporting oppression by unwittingly voicing false consciousness which keeps oppressors in power and thwarts justice, the critic must prove moral innocence as well as adduce acceptable evidence. There will be little serious discourse so long as this part of the current theological scene requires confession of sin and conversion before a serious conversation can begin.

The third consequence is not yet an actuality but a real danger. Until now, the transformation of theology into legitimation for political action has had a clear leftist cast, but what prevents using the same warrants and slogans to promote reactionary right-wing politics? Nothing at all. There are only historical—that is, circumstantial—reasons why thus far the theological trend has developed in the name of liberating women, minorities, and the destitute from their plight. But fascism has shown that one can appeal to justice and equity to support also a revolution of the right, because all one must do is to redefine the aggrieved.

Fourth, in some theological education the goal of alienation-driven theology is not developing the capacity for independent thinking grounded in a solid grasp of the tradition, but empowerment. When the goal is power, whether to hold it or to gain it, the quest for truth is an early casualty. The more theology becomes politicized, the less possible

---

23. Jane Schaberg, *The Illegitimacy of Jesus: A Feminist Theological Interpretation of the Infancy Narratives* (San Francisco: Harper & Row, 1987).

becomes an unprejudiced examination of the issues—precisely what is needed most in our day. Without that, research becomes a hunt for data to support indoctrination, a sure sign that intellectual life is no longer self-correcting and that independent thought has fled.

Just as multiple changes in weather patterns produce a changed climate, for which no single storm is responsible, so these changes have had a cumulative impact on the churches. Can anyone deny that the theological climate is a factor in the decline and shrinkage of the mainline churches? The first chapter called attention to the lack of interest of the crucial group—the young adults. Many of them desire an alternative both to fundamentalism's intellectual rigor mortis and to assorted mainline mixtures of religious uncertainty and political certainty, but they find a void at the center. Those who turn to conservative churches want more than simple and safe answers—the usual self-serving explanation in mainline circles. In the midst of religious and moral chaos, these folk seek a faith that has been tested and found true enough by ample Christian experience for them to live by, to transmit to their children, and to commend shamelessly to their friends. They sense that a hermeneutic of suspicion is essential if the churches are to come to terms with their past, but they also sense that unless the hermeneutic of alienation is replaced by a hermeneutic of affirmation, the churches will continue to drift, lacking conviction and confidence. And they are right.

A Hermeneutic of Affirmation

If mainline Protestantism is to be renewed, developing a hermeneutic of affirmation is as essential as recovering the praise of God in worship. This hermeneutic needs to be characterized briefly.

To begin with, the hermeneutic of affirmation is *not* a substitute for the hermeneutic of suspicion, for we can neither turn our backs on what it has taught us about the formation of the Christian tradition and its function in society, nor accept without murmur everything handed to us from the past. Instead, the hermeneutic of suspicion and the hermeneutic of affirmation belong *together*, sometimes functioning sequentially, sometimes dialectically. The hermeneutic of affirmation is rather like the so-called second naivete Paul Ricoeur emphasized. A hermeneutic of affirmation is neither another "new theology," of which we have had enough, nor a particular "old" theology restored as part of a return to an idealized past. If the hermeneutic of suspicion has made anything clear, it is that there was no Golden Age which must be restored, not even the first century. We are already more like the early Christians than we ought to be.

Positively, a hermeneutic of affirmation will reclaim, renew, and release critically the classical Christian tradition into the life of the churches, where it can find its own level of influence by clarifying their identity and mission on the one hand, and by generating a vision of a new Christian humanism on the other. This tradition is not a neatly marked system. Its boundaries are seldom precise. It is more like the Mississippi than a concrete-lined irrigation canal. It is a patterned way of thinking, like a style of music various composers can adapt while it remains recognizably itself.

A hermeneutic of affirmation claims the legacy of our forebears despite their blind spots in matters of social justice important to us, because much of what they did see they saw more clearly than we, who have our own blind spots, which our successors will not hesitate to point out (and write dissertations about). The hermeneutic of affirmation is at least as willing to learn from our predecessors as it is to teach them what their faults were. The hermeneutic of affirmation is a persistent but pained loyalty to a heritage, which, though flawed, nonetheless has given us what faith we have and which is supple enough to survive what we will do to it. Like the hermeneutic of suspicion and of alienation, it is not a theory but a stance, not a procedure but a disposition to say, "Yes, despite . . . " It accepts the task of thinking with our forebears where we can and against them where we must.

Affirmation and Renewal

But does the renewal of mainline Protestantism really depend on developing a hermeneutic of affirmation? I believe it does, and for two reasons.

First of all, to renew churches, not clubs, political parties, or special interest groups, is to revitalize what has been constitutive of their existence—response to the gospel and its perduring theological infrastructure. Renewed communities change, but rarely by lurching or by repudiating the identities formed by their histories. They change by assimilating some of the new and abandoning some of the old, not always quietly or painlessly. Ordaining women and providing them access to positions of leadership in the mainline churches is a clear example of this process. Communities that are being renewed value their continuities because they enable them to assimilate change with confidence. A hermeneutic of affirmation is the stance that makes lasting change possible for the church confident.

In the second place, the hermeneutic of suspicion alone cannot provide renewal, for the various critical methods and procedures it spawned were designed for quite different purposes—to assess the validity of the church's traditions, whether about the authorship of the Pentateuch or the Jerusalem church. Indeed, we very much need a thorough study of the history of biblical interpretation showing how the hermeneutic of suspicion and its consequences actually functioned in the churches' use of the Bible. That would show, I suspect, that the hermeneutic of suspicion func-

tioned most fruitfully when it operated in tandem with a
hermeneutic of affirmation, once largely taken for granted.
Be that as it may, just as astute use of historical criticism will
not make one a better Christian, so relying on the
hermeneutic of suspicion alone will not, and cannot, renew
the churches. It can be renewal's John the Baptist, but it
cannot be its messiah. Nor will reliance on the hermeneutic
of affirmation alone renew the churches, for that would lead
to reassertion without reform. But if the churches will use
both hermeneutics, they can be both self-critical and confident.

Whether that will occur depends, in large part, on their
leaders. Renewal and reform repeatedly have started from
preachers who became theologians because their work drove
them ever deeper into the heart of the Christian faith.
Friedrich Schleiermacher, Jonathan Edwards, John Wesley,
Nathaniel Taylor, Horace Bushnell, Karl Barth, Reinhold
Niebuhr, Martin Luther King, Jr.—preachers they were first.
If that says anything, it says that there will be no renewal of
theology in the churches until theology is renewed in the
pulpits.

Eighty-five years ago, another Beecher lecturer made the
same point, noting that because people do not know where
they are, they steer "by reckoning—when anything can happen." Then, with his eye to solar navigation he added: "But
theology is 'taking the sun.' And it is wonderful . . . how few
of our officers can use the sextant for themselves. Yet what is
the use of captains who are more at home entertaining the
passengers than navigating the ship?"[24] Too long have
churches and their leaders understood themselves as con-
sumers of "new theology" produced by professionals in aca-
deme, important as they may be. Too long have seminaries
vitiated their talk about teaching future preachers to "think

---

24. P. T. Forsyth, *Positive Preaching and the Modern Mind*, p. 101.

theologically" by encouraging them to sample everything in the cafeteria lest the latest be missed. Too long have pastoring preachers avoided the court of theological accountability by pleading guilty to the lesser charge of busyness.

Where is one to begin? Where pastors already are and with what they are already doing—in the study and in the pulpit, where one wrestles with the truth about the God who is praised in Christian worship. Academic theologians can renew theology *for* the churches, but it is preachers grappling with the meaning of the faith for today who will renew it *in* the churches. And isn't that where it really belongs?

CHAPTER THREE

ETHOS

Ministers are conceived of as professionals, and a church is known by activities it keeps. A good church is a panting church.

—Leonard Sweet, "Can a Mainstream Change Its Course?"

Though modern Americans may differ in many particulars from their Puritan and evangelical ancestors, they are still deeply committed to working out their own salvation, and the salvation of everyone else, through the restructuring of public life.

—Mark Noll, *One Nation Under God?*

Creation, *not* the state, is a theocracy.

—Aidan Kavanagh, *On Liturgical Theology*

The churches should *inform* the ethos and conscience of the nation, and thus aid in forming the conscience of its statesmen.

—Paul Ramsey, *Who Speaks for the Church?*

If anything makes it clear that the mainline churches need renewal that reforms, it is their continuing conflict over their role in public life. This conflict is driven partly by the gnawing sense that just as their membership has hemorrhaged, so their standing in society has gone from importance to impotence. While their decline in size has produced some anxiety, in some quarters the rising influence of evangelicals has caused sheer panic. The role of all churches in our society has changed, but the mainliners' traditional concern for public affairs makes a new self-understanding particularly pressing for them. After noting briefly the changed circumstances, we will explore alternatives and then make some suggestions.

The Loss of the Protestant Franchise

Despite the best human efforts to make history—that is, to make it come out right—usually history happens to us. The turning points, the pivotal changes, do not occur because we planned or scheduled them, but result from the interaction of many factors that we do not foresee and cannot control. No one planned the Protestant Reformation, the discovery of the two continents west of Europe and Africa, the slaughter that two worldwide wars turned out to be, or the collapse of the Soviet Union. The winds of history blow as they will, bringing the unexpected to pass and summoning us to adjust our sails as best we can. So too, no one planned the relentless and irreversible pluralization of the American populace, which is taking us ever farther from the Puritan goal of the kingdom of God in America.

Despite the steady pluralization which began in the nineteenth century, until recently the ethos of the nation was shaped by Protestantism, especially by the mainliners, who, as Harvard's William Hutchison observes, "felt responsible for America: for its moral structure, for the religious content of national ideals, for the education and welfare functions that government would not (or, it was thought, should not) carry out."[1] In other words, these churches exercised a "custodianship" even though "No church leaders have ever been authorized as the official spokesmen of the Christian conscience of the American nation" as the British historian, David Edwards, notes.[2]

Apart from the disastrous failure of Prohibition, the achievements of this informal establishment were considerable, though it is now fashionable for liberal Protestants to feel guilty for once having exercised a certain hegemony, which Martin Marty has called "the righteous empire."[3]

Whether we feel guilty or nostalgic, that era cannot be restored. Twenty years ago Sydney Ahlstrom's magisterial *Religious History of the American People* not only titled its introductory chapter "American Religion in the Post-Protestant Era," but also observed that "only in the 1960's would it become apparent that the Great Puritan epoch in American history had come to an end."[4] That might have been premature because important continuities remain as well, as John Wilson at Princeton insists.[5] Indeed, Laurence Moore has noted that declaring the death of Protestant dominance itself has an interesting history.[6] In the same vein, William Clebsch contended that Protestants have rarely felt good about their real achievements because their originally religiously motivated institutions later "belonged no longer to

1. William R. Hutchison, "Preface: From Protestant to Pluralist America," *Between the Times,* p. viii.

2. David L. Edwards, *The Futures of Christianity,* p. 128.

3. Martin E. Marty published a book bearing this title in 1970. In the revised edition, "Righteous Empire" became the subtitle for *Protestantism in the United States.*

4. Sydney Ahlstrom, *A Religious History of the American People,* p. 35.

5. John F. Wilson, "Religion at the Core of American Culture," in Lotz, *Altered Landscapes,* pp. 362-76.

6. *Religious Outsiders,* p. viii.

the saints but to the citizenry," prompting prophets to cry that "the success of the church signalled the failure of the gospel."[7]

In any case, one reason there is chaos in the churches and confusion in the land is that while the Puritan era may have ended, the Puritan idea continues in the determination to Christianize America. What Puritan Urien Oakes, once President of Harvard College, described (perhaps naively) we still want: Said Oakes, "The interest of righteousness in the commonwealth and the holiness in the church are inseparable. . . . Christ reigns among us in the commonwealth as well as in the churches."[8] Centuries later, Walter Rauschenbusch titled one of his books *Christianizing the Social Order.* As late as 1950, at the founding of the National Council of Churches, Bishop Sherill's sermon declared that the Council's creation "marks a new and great determination that the American way will be increasingly the Christian way, for such is our heritage. . . . Together the churches can move forward to the goal of a Christian America in a Christian world."[9] He obviously did not consult his Jewish and Muslim neighbors.[10]

Today it is hard to imagine a time when the churches had the active support of the elite. John D. Rockefeller was an active churchman and philanthropist, the patron of the new University of Chicago. John R. Mott, missionary leader and head of the once highly significant Student Volunteer Movement, knew nine Presidents, and on one day in 1923 met with former President Taft in the morning, had lunch with President Coolidge, and visited former President Wilson in

---

7. William A. Clebsch, *From Sacred to Profane America,* pp. 3, 9.

8. Quoted from Ahlstrom, *A Religious History of the American People,* p. 198.

9. Quoted from Robert A. Schneider, "Voice of Many Waters: Church Federation in the Twentieth Century," in Hutchison, *Between the Times,* p. 117.

10. Richard L. Rubenstein claims that "the basic strategy of the Jewish community in modern times has been, wherever possible, withdrawal from Christian influence." Quoted from Wilson and Drakeman, eds., *Church and State in American History,* pp. 182-83.

the afternoon.[11] Today, only Billy Graham could match that, and if he did, it would make the mainliners both nervous and envious. In the late nineteenth century, mainline clergy dominated the college boards of trust, but already by 1926 their number had declined markedly at schools like Yale and Princeton.[12] Today, clergy are almost completely absent from the boards of trust of such schools—reflecting not simply secularization but also the general decline in the stature of the clergy. The establishment people knew one another, worked together, and marshaled resources to support the activities of the churches. Today many rejoice because the increased role of women, minorities, and Catholics has destroyed the old white male Protestant elite. Yet, something important has been lost—a cadre of strong leaders, with real followers, who knew how to work together within a common framework of understanding and commitment, which, while pervasively Protestant, was not narrowly so but broadly Christian. In its place is an elite of another kind—the church bureaucrats often more responsive to the leaders of particular constituencies and caucuses, the sachems of special interests, than to the churches as a whole.[13]

The main point is that in ever larger areas of our country, the Protestant—indeed the Christian—franchise has expired; it will not be renewed. Only tyranny can restore it. The future is less and less like the past. What, then, are the options?

---

11. William R. Hutchison, "Protestantism as Establishment," in Hutchison, *Between the Times,* p. 7 (quoting C. Howard Hopkins' biography of Mott).

12. According to Dorothy C. Bass, "Between 1884 and 1926 the number of clergy trustees declined by 50% at Amherst, 60% at Yale, and 67% at Princeton; at fifteen other private colleges, clergy trustees declined from 39% in 1860 to 23% in 1900 to 7% in 1930." She also notes the disappearance of clergy from the presidencies of Harvard (1869), Yale (1899), Princeton (1902), and Oberlin (1927). "Ministry on the Margin: Protestants and Education," in Hutchison, *Between the Times,* p. 57.

13. For a good discussion of this phenomenon of church bureaucracies, *see* Conrad Wright, "The Growth of Denominational Bureaucracies: A Neglected Aspect of American Church History," *Harvard Theological Review* 77 (1984): 177-94.

Options for the Future

Unsatisfactory Images

One alternative is to go countercultural, to become churches committed to being a cluster of resistance movements in a society seen as pervasively hostile to the truth of the gospel no matter how benign it makes itself appear. A counterculture church will be determined to be pure church above all. The desire to go countercultural, to be a subversive church, is of a piece with the hermeneutic of alienation, which was discussed briefly in the foregoing chapter. The continuity between the hermeneutic of alienation, which puts virtually the whole Christian tradition on the defensive, and the demand for a countercultural church should not surprise us, for the mindset is the same. In fact, ideologically, this view of church and society is but the religious left-wing mirror image of the neo-Nazi groups on the right, though they are alienated from opposite things. In ecclesiology, this alienation drives people to look ceaselessly for a perfect church, one that is so intent on being the body of *Christ* that it forgets that it is also Christ's *body*—a historically contingent, empirical community that is frail, vulnerable to disease, and more given to flabbiness than to Schwarzeneggerish muscle tone. Nor should it surprise us if the countercultural church, having demonized non-Christian elements in society, can scarcely avoid living in a Manichaean world, where the Redeemer is not the Creator but the Creator's adversary.

While some voices within the mainline churches call for a countercultural stance in the name of true discipleship, it is altogether unlikely that these churches will heed them. Their whole history makes them tone deaf to such a summons. Besides, most people prefer to be for something and not primarily against the society in which they live, and they prefer making a contribution to it instead of trying to subvert it. In a word, a countercultural stance is for the mainliners not a real option.

A less radical option, proposed recently by Stanley Hauerwas and William Willimon, sees the church as resident alien.[14] This option is more attractive to those not alienated in principle, because it contends that the church must do its own thing. The resident alien church is more concerned to be authentic than to be pure. And for its beat it listens to the Bible and the Christian tradition rather than the pounding rhythms around it.

Unfortunately, however, this accent is inappropriate for the mainline churches. The image of "resident aliens" is at best ambiguous, for while some resident aliens do participate in public life, many others merely cluster together to perpetuate the ways of "the old country." Indeed, Hauerwas and Willimon virtually endorse the latter style when they suggest that "the church is a colony, an island of one culture in the middle of another" (p. 12); that implies that the church is to American society what the missionary compound once was to Chinese culture. Curiously, such a view virtually describes, unwittingly to be sure, the megachurches, which provide everything for their constituents but housing and jobs—a world within a world.

The third stance is not really an option but a trend already under way, namely, a social activism grounded in the assumption that the church must be the avant-garde of leftward social change—the flip side of the rightward assumption that it should be the vanguard of the restoration of Christendom. Controversies over public policy matters are so intense because knowingly or not both antagonists are struggling for control of the same legacy—the right to shape American society according to God's will, about whose con-

---

14. Stanley Hauerwas and William H. Willimon, *Resident Aliens.*

tent there is ever less agreement.[15] Since the rightward restoration is precluded apart from a tyranny, which no one wants, the leftward lure has enough of an appeal that it merits brief comment.

This avant-garde model summons the churches to solidarity with those efforts to change society which have been identified as the places where God is at work, a discernment that makes participation in them at least as mandatory as anything in the New Testament. Moreover, this view of the church in society is inevitably utilitarian, for it sees the church's life and work, including the worship of God, as preparation for involvement in what really matters—social struggle. One thing should not escape notice here: The advocates of this view of church in society have rejected that model of societies that sees them as functioning well because they have achieved a degree of equilibrium, a certain integration of roles; instead, they have chosen that model which sees societies as engaged in conflict. Further, the question is not whether Christians should involve themselves in efforts to change the destructive conditions in which many people now live but whether the churches ought to do so as churches, and if so, on what basis? In other words, What is church? This is, in fact, the question to which Peter L. Berger has called attention:

> The public postures of the major churches . . . [are increasingly] nothing but near-automatic reflexes of the class cultures to which their leaders belong or aspire.[16] I don't think

15. Leonard Sweet puts it sharply: "The inability of modernist churches [the mainliners] to create a popular consensus for their policies meant that they had to rely increasingly on undemocratic means to achieve democratic ends. Li'tle wonder that church bureaucracies became disturbed for being out of touch with the people, that an anti-establishment spirit emerged in all modernist churches, and that religious alternatives to denominations proved more and more attractive" ("The Modernization of Protestant Religion in America," in Lotz, *Altered Landscapes,* p. 31).

16. Berger alludes to the new class as the opinion-makers and rising professionals. *See* chap. 2, n. 14.

that chaplaincy in a class war is the proper function of Christian ministry to society. . . . When political partisanship becomes a routine feature of the church's public role . . . the most serious consequence is that the church loses one of its defining marks, that of *catholicity*: It ceases to be the church.[17]

This avante-garde ecclesiology is of a piece with the secularization of worship noted in the first chapter, for the symptom of secularized worship is anthropocentrism; its offspring is the utilitarian mind, which sees everything in terms of benefits. Once the church defines itself as the change agent for justice, people soon discover that the goals of social change can be pursued, and perhaps reached, without the gospel or the church. Indeed, Hauerwas and Willimon point out that "activist Christians who talk much about justice promote a notion of justice that envisions a society in which faith in God is rendered quite unnecessary, since everybody already believes in peace and justice even when everybody does not believe in God."[18] In other words, down this road, the activist church becomes the *useful* church, and then finds that in order to remain truly useful it must become either a *pure* church brooking no compromise or a *secularized* church which has forfeited its raison d'être.

In the long run, none of these alternatives is viable. As noted, the "righteous empire" cannot be restored. The mainliners' long and honorable involvement in public affairs makes the call to become countercultural appealing only to the alienated among them who find in our society much to condemn and little to affirm. The leftward bent of the activist model threatens to make the churches irrelevant and impotent as communities of faith, either by diluting the faith or by abetting an institutionalization of the churches—

---

17. "American Religion" in Michaelson, *Liberal Protestantism*, p. 35.
18. *Resident Aliens*, p. 37.

already far advanced—by turning them into holding corporations for assorted and conflicting causes, because only institutional allegiance will allow the contending commitments and causes to co-exist in churches committed to being inclusive. And a truly inclusive church either becomes a replica of a pluralist secular society or a sect composed of those who agree on a particular kind of inclusivism.[19]

Rethinking Basics: Theocracy and Messianism

A more viable future entails reconsidering thoroughly the assumptions that have been the foundation of the ethos the mainline churches inherited but which the course of history has now made inoperable. Put simply, the mainline churches must free themselves from the notion that they have a God-given responsibility for society, and instead claim the freedom to become influential participants in society by being first of all accountable to the gospel. Making such a move requires rigorous exegetical and theological work, for virtually the whole of Christian theology will be on the table before the task is completed. Here, however, it must suffice to identify two areas where such work should begin. The first entails renunciation, the second reconstruction.

What must be renounced, once and for all, *is the theocratic ideal,* even though it was fundamental in ancient Israel and through Scripture became basic in the Calvinist model of church and society which many mainliners inherited and still perpetuate. Ancient Israel took for granted that the king rules in God's name so that society would function in accord with the divine will within the covenant framework. In that

---

19. Leonard Sweet exaggerates only slightly when he observes that in recent years "pluralism [inclusiveness] became the fairy godmother of modernist Protestantism, non-inclusiveness its wicked stepfather" ("The Modernization of Protestant Religion in America," in Lotz, *Altered Landscapes,* p. 36).

culture, it was also assumed that the prophets were God's messengers who had not only a religious obligation but a civil right to rebuke society for its injustices and to hold the king himself accountable to God. Although there were also court prophets on government payrolls, the prophets we read in Scripture often opposed the king, and for the most part got away with it because both prophet and king functioned within a theocratic framework. The prophets functioned in that culture more like a mullah in Iran than a mainline preacher in America today.

Through Calvinism, the influence of this theocratic model has been so pervasive and so persistent that neither the legal disestablishment of the churches nor the famous wall of separation between church and state has been able to quell the churches' insatiable thirst for theocratic power.[20] The theocratic ideal persists despite a pluralism which neither Israel nor Calvin could have foreseen and which they might well have repudiated if they had. In pluralist America, even if the churches could agree on what a Christian America would look like, and even if they deem it imperative to speak a prophetic word, as on occasion they rightly do, they cannot escalate their built-in right to be *heard* into a right to be *heeded*.

To some elements in the mainline churches, the call to renounce the theocratic ideal may seem like a summons to suicide. Actually, however, the course of our history has already made giving it up a matter of ratifying the obvious. History has returned us to a status rather like that of the pre-

---

20. A quarter century ago Paul Ramsey, in criticizing those who affirmed that the church had become a sect in a world "come of age" and still identified Christian social ethics with public policy formation, observed: "The oddity is that contemporary ecumenical social ethics evidences less acknowledgement of the separation between the church and the office of magistrate and citizen than was clearly acknowledged by the great cultural churches of the past—except perhaps by the claims made by the bull *Unam Sanctum* (Boniface VIII, November 18, 1302)" (*Who Speaks for the Church?* p. 20).

Constantinian church. That church found its vocation without the theocratic ideal, and in many parts of the modern world the churches have done so again. There is no reason why the mainline churches cannot do so in this country as well. We need not regard theocracy as an egregious error, or denounce the Constantinian symbiosis of church and state as the great betrayal, for the creation of a Christianized civilization in Europe was a magnificent achievement, despite instances of terrible misuse of power. Nor does the surrender of the theocratic ideal entail the creation of a conventicle church that is no longer concerned with our common life in society, for it is one thing to have influence for good, another to have power to impose it.

The second task before us is *reconstruction of Christology by severing it from messianism.* This will surely be more difficult, but the very difficulty shows how essential it is to make this disconnection real. At issue is nothing less than what it means and does not mean to call Jesus the Christ, the Messiah.

On this task some basic historical considerations must be brought to bear. To begin with, recent reexamination of the evidence has exposed the extent to which Christian thinking has skewed the portrayal of the Jewish context of Jesus and the earliest church: (a) Not only were there a number of "Judaisms" before the destruction of Jerusalem in 70 C.E., but the rabbinism that emerged subsequently also differed from the Pharisaism that preceded it. (b) Accordingly, one should not speak of "the Jewish hope for a Messiah," since not every group expected one; some texts expected God to bring salvation and ignore a messianic hope altogether. (c) Those who did expect a messiah had no standard view of his role, and the Dead Sea Scroll community expected two messiahs, one a priest and the other a kingly figure. (d) In some texts, to be sure, the messiah was to be the key God-given solution to the frustrated hopes of theocracy—the nation's deliverer and ideal ruler of a just society.[21]

Moreover, whether or not Jesus regarded himself as the messiah, from the start Christians believed that the hope for a messiah had been made actual in the rather non-messianic Jesus. Further, within two decades Paul was using the Greek word "Christ" as if it were Jesus' last name. But in Paul's Christology almost nothing remains of the messianic. Not one of his references to the future coming of the Lord Jesus, the *parousia*, mentions or assumes clearly that the Lord Jesus will rule a righteous kingdom on earth. In fact, the only book in the New Testament that clearly expects this to occur is the book of Revelation, which Robert Jewett holds largely responsible for American religious zealotry.[22] Those early believers who incorporated Jesus into their messianism did not give the basic beat for what became classical Christology.

In short, once the earliest Christians believed that Jesus' resurrection signaled the inbreaking of the Age to Come, it was inevitable that a whole range of titles and categories linked with the bringer of salvation were attached to him. But it was the shape and the quality of Jesus' life and the character of the salvation experienced that provided the

---

21. These matters are amply discussed in the volume of studies edited by Jacob Neusner, William S. Green, and Ernest Frerichs, *Judaisms and Their Messiahs at the Turn of the Christian Era.*

22. Robert Jewett, *The Captain America Complex.* Jewett sees two contradictory strands in the Bible: zealous nationalism and prophetic realism (the Old Testament prophets and Jesus). Jesus' message, he holds, was interpreted by posterity in light of Deuteronomy (the triumph of the righteous), Daniel and worst of all Revelation, which "placed its stamp on the whole Bible" by "submerging the strand of Prophetic Realism . . . under the grandiose flood of zealous images and ideas" of God's triumph over opponents "who are stereotyped as bestial and irredeemable." As a result "the book of Revelation provided a mythic framework for a mission of the [American] nation" (pp. 24-26), including "the Grand Conspiracy" view of recent history (pp. 116-20). The role of the Apocalypse in the American self-image deserves more careful investigation than Jewett's sketch is able to give it. Still, it is odd that he does not mention at all the role of messianism—nor the role of persecution and martyrdom in shaping the horizon of apocalyptic thought.

actual content of their Christology, not Jewish messianic ideas. The title "Christ" fits Jesus because its meaning was rebuilt so that it would.[23] Thereby the Christian messiah Jesus was separated from Jewish messianism, and in principle from all messianism as well. It is time to acknowledge this achievement, and to be grateful for it. Our world has had enough messiahs.

It should be clear that by "messianism" I mean not the habit of calling Jesus "Christ" but the fervent expectation that God's agent will, either through divine intervention alone or through collaboration with human efforts, end the reign of wickedness and in its place establish in history the reign of God. In other words, messianism is nothing other than eschatological theocracy—that is, the conviction that some figure or group will make real the theocratic ideal as the goal of history because it is God's will. Moreover, God can count on us to do our part—and maybe part of God's as well. In our century, the wholly secularized messianism which has captivated many moderns is communism. And understandably, for messianism promises paradise on earth and in history. For the highly secularized, such a this-worldly, historically actual salvation is the only kind one can expect.

What is at stake in deleting messianism from Christology and from faith in Christ is now clear: It is nothing less than the nature of salvation and the role of a community that looks to Jesus as its head. A messianist church either becomes ever more imperialist as it strives to make real a specifically Christian theocracy, or ever more secular because the Utopia is achievable in a pluralist world only by declining to be explicitly Christian. What is *not* at stake in

---

23. The use of "messianism" here is narrower and more precise than Jürgen Moltmann's facile appropriation of "messianic" to characterize Jesus and the church. This is not, however, the forum in which to sort out the issues (*The Church in the Power of the Spirit*, pp. 76-85).

deleting messianism is the freedom, right, and responsibility of Christians to do what they can to bring about a more just world. In fact, we are freer to engage in such efforts without the baggage of messianism than with it, because only messianists must succeed.

Having explored all too briefly the negative side of the thesis—the liberation of the churches from the theocratic end and its messianic means—we now turn to the positive side: freedom for a responsible participation in our pluralist society by being first of all accountable to the gospel. Unless this accountability has clear priority, participation in society will be driven by some combination of prudence and the passion that has haunted liberal Protestantism from the start—the passion to be "with it."

Being first accountable to the gospel is nothing other than a consequence of developing a hermeneutic of affirmation. This accountability implies that the churches know that neither their perception of the gospel nor their fidelity to it can be taken for granted, but must be reassessed repeatedly. The point is that in a pluralist society significant participation requires the churches to be true to themselves as communities responding to the Good News. Otherwise their participation becomes ever more superfluous.

What is being considered here is the participation of the mainline churches, not of mainline Christians. The two must not be conflated or confused even if they are inseparable. That there is often a tension between the order of the institution and the ardor of the individual is clear enough; nonetheless, it is within the institutional order that the individual's ardor is generated, nurtured, and sustained.

What, then, is a viable vocation for the mainline churches—one that no longer commits adultery in the heart by lusting after the power of the state to impose messianist goals, on the one hand, and that does not covet the purity of a sect engaged in guerrilla warfare against society, on the other?

In Pluralism, Influence

Instead of being a community of resident aliens who, like some refugee and immigrant communities, enjoy the advantage of residence while eschewing public life, this vocation entails *commitment to being a long-range influence for the common good.* The image that comes to mind is that of dual citizenship, for that points to the necessary and inevitable tension that exists between loyalty to society and loyalty to the kingdom of God.[24] Identifying several possibilities will suggest what such a vocation might look like in a pluralistic world.

Since what is in view here are illustrative possibilities for the long-term influence of the churches as public institutions, the activities expressing the cup of water ministries require no discussion; besides, Christians respond to suffering and need whether their society is pluralist or homogeneous. So too, the perspective of long-term influence leaves aside activities, pro or con, which involve specific legislation. What is in view here are possible modes of having a positive influence in society by what the church does and says week in and week out, for it is by patient and persistent pursuit of the ordinary that attitudes are formed and understandings are matured. Renewed and confident churches know that in the long run the character and quality of their steady routine is more significant than a frenetic 911 style. Two roles allow the churches to exert a long-range influence.

The Public Theologian

First, the churches can play the role of public theologian, clarifying, affirming, interpreting, and scrutinizing the deep-

---

24. The image of dual citizenship is comparable to the Lutheran doctrine of "two kingdoms," which has often been misread as sanctioning bifurcation of the sacred and secular, and as justifying quietism in the public realm. But making a distinction between what promotes the common good of all and what is distinctly Christian is by no means the same as ignoring the former in order to be absorbed by the latter. The whole theme merits a rethinking. For a starter, *see* Carl E. Braaten, "The Doctrine of Two Kingdoms Reexamined," in *Justification,* pp. 171-82.

est impulses of our society, on the assumption that other kinds of Christians, as well as Jews, Muslims, those of other faiths, and those professing no religion, will do the same. Although the role of public theologian is many-sided, three aspects deserve discussion.

First, the churches can develop and state a robust and realistic theology of politics and of political power, including a theology of law informed by Paul's anthropology. Much of today's theology is preoccupied with the distribution of power, evidently assuming that it is an unambiguous good which needs only to be shared more widely. The problem is not with the goal but with the romantic view of power. Given the power of vast bureaucracies of every sort, on the one hand, and the exercise of power by nation-states large and small, on the other, few things are more important than a clear-headed, unromantic, theologically sound view of power. In developing such, the mainline churches have a moral obligation to admit that in their eagerness to restructure American society through politics, they have both condoned and abetted a growth of governmental power so enormous that it leaves no aspect of life untouched. Government and its bureaucracies have become our saviors, and any attempt to question their place often evokes the same response Paul got in Ephesus: "Great is Diana!"

A more clear-headed perspective will insist that power cannot solve problems of inequity without limiting freedom, because freedom leads to inequality, and equality can be enforced only by tyranny.[25] The reason for this is in the

---

25. Reinhold Niebuhr saw this clearly: Because all communities have hierarchies, "equality" is an essential criterion of criticism; conversely, because all communities' cohesion relies on various forces (from kinship to police), "liberty" is also essential. Referring to seventeenth-century British experience, he observes: "Neither the libertarians nor the equalitarians realized that equality and liberty are in paradoxical relation to each other and that it is possible to maintain the one only at the price of the other" ("Liberty and Equality," in *Pious and Secular America*, p. 69).

nature of the human heart and will. Paul's anthropology accounts not only for this tension between equality and freedom but also for the fact that although law is essential in making us act fairly and civilly, it cannot coerce the human heart into goodness or prevent people from perverting its ends for their own self-interest.

When the churches are emancipated from theocratic and messianist notions they can also develop a more secular view of politics. Only if we understand politics as the struggle for power can we desacralize it. Whatever else that the church can and should say about political life, it must say clearly that pluralism accentuates politics as a struggle for power; that governments, like politicians, normally make primary the continuance and legitimation of their power; that Caesar never lives by the Sermon on the Mount; that although the struggle for power may be motivated by religion it is not itself a religious process but a thoroughly secular one; that nonetheless it is not autonomous but subject to moral judgment.

This judgment, though rooted in specifically Christian convictions, is expressible in and consistent with elemental moral values that are widely accepted. Cardinal Bernardin once said that "religiously rooted positions must somehow be translated into language, arguments and categories which a religiously pluralistic society can agree on as the moral foundation of key policy positions."[26] If that be granted, then Protestant and Catholic theology should join in the quest for an adequate equivalent of natural law, difficult as this will be. Without something like natural law, the warrants for the moral judgments the churches make about the political process, or any other public matter, will have no influence on the public mind.

Mark Noll notes that to a large extent American Christian

26. Quoted from Richard P. McBrien, *Caesar's Coin*, p. 126.

attitudes toward politics can be traced to the nineteenth-century revivals, especially as conducted and interpreted by Charles G. Finney. According to Noll, Finney and the revivals were immediatist (offering salvation now), ultraist (demanding that everything be set aside to pursue it), and perfectionist (brooking no compromise).[27] This legacy helps us understand why the churches have implied that politics, especially elections, are religious crusades against evil, have promised salvation, have allowed one issue to demand complete allegiance, and have viewed compromise as betrayal. In other words, messianism provided the goal, revivalist legacy the power. By not infusing our political process with such religious, messianist fervor the churches would be an influence for the common good. Then the nation might desist from regarding its foreign affairs and wars as crusades while being amazed that Muslim fundamentalists still talk of a jihad.

The second aspect of our common life which the mainline churches can illumine theologically for the benefit of all is anthropology—what we believe about ourselves and our salvation. When Yale's R. W. B. Lewis coined the phrase "the American Adam," he saw the point,[28] though he is not responsible for my reading of Adam.[29] The American Adam is both innocent and perfectible because he did not experience the "Fall" and so has no significant complicity in the evils that beset him; rather he is an innocent victim who, if but liberated from the evil structures imposed by society, and from the malign influence of neurotic parents, will

---

27. Mark A. Noll, *One Nation Under God?* pp. 108-11, 158.

28. R. W. B. Lewis, *The American Adam: Innocence, Tragedy, and Tradition in the Nineteenth Century* (Chicago: University of Chicago Press, 1955).

29. William A. Dyrness, I find, also uses "the American Adam," though somewhat differently, calling attention not only to the themes of individualism and perfectibility but also to client-centered counseling (*How Does America Hear the Gospel?* chap. 5).

flourish and perfect himself by actualizing all his possibilities. So long as his acts do not infringe too much on another person's rights, anything is permitted that fulfills him. This Adam can be a loner or a joiner, for he is an autonomous person, whose social relationships are a matter of contract—arrangements that can be made, changed, unmade, as needed or desired. For the American Adam, the word "God" is a symbol for the power that is available for pursuing one's goals. His offspring are not Cain and Abel, or Moses viewing Canaan from afar, but Ralph Waldo Emerson and Horatio Alger.

Seeing ourselves as the American Adam has produced ambiguous results. It has, to be sure, nourished a naive optimism and persistent idealism, which propelled a society that is never content with its achievements. And there are enough Horatio Alger stories, especially among immigrants, to give this Adam some credibility. But the destructive consequences are there too. The unqualified individualism has given us rights without responsibilities and has undermined basic human bonds, including the family as a social unit in which loyalty, self-control, and mutual good are learned and character built. This Adam is now burdened by enormous guilt, on the one hand, for succeeding in the past by nearly exterminating Native Americans along with native bison, and, on the other hand, for not succeeding in the present. We condemn ourselves as failures if our bodies are not slim, if we are not perfect parents, if our children are not achievers too, if we do not get promoted continually. In short, if you have problems with your life, it's probably your fault. And while there is truth in that, it is haunted by illusions.

The mainline churches know that the biblical Adam is the real one, even in America. They know that the real Adam is an accomplice in his own undoing, that he perverts the good while pursuing it, that his impulses are somewhat contain-

able and improvable but not perfectible, that a fulfilled
Adam is a distorted self because, being social by nature, he
has absorbed the habits of mind and action that were developed east of Eden where all history takes place; they know
that he can fly to the moon but cannot flee himself. In a
word, by unmasking the illusions about ourselves, the
churches can be a positive influence on the mindset of the
nation and thereby mitigate the frustration and despair that
comes from expecting the impossible of ourselves.

The third aspect of the churches' role as theologian
invites them to relate the American saga to transcendent
perspectives. Cultural anthropologists point out that one
important function of religion is to articulate a plausibility
structure, a legitimating story or myth, which expresses
the people's identity and place in the world. Until recently,
Protestant Christianity provided much of this story, which,
according to John Wilson, came to have two versions—
America as exemplar (the Puritan image of the New Zion,
the city on the hill), and America as emissary with a mission to be the savior of democracy;[30] Charles Mabee had
the same thing in mind when he wrote of the mythos of
exceptionality and the mythos of mission.[31] The presence
of the American flag in many churches symbolized the role
of Christianity in supporting both visions of ourselves. It is
not accidental that the discussion of "civil religion"
emerged just when elements of American society—the
alienated elite opinion-makers at the top and those at the
bottom who felt left out of the story—announced that they
no longer believed the story and excoriated those who did.
The turmoil in our society shows that we no longer have
what every coherent society has—a framework, a common
set of symbols, an umbrella story that puts American aspi-

---

30. John F. Wilson, *Public Religion in American Culture*, chap. 2.

31. Charles Mabee, *Reimaging America*, pp. 27-31.

ration and experience in a perspective that is shared widely.[32]

Today, the field is wide open for the formation of a revisionist legitimation story that provides a chastened sense of identity and meaning to the American people. Precisely here, however, the mainline opinion-makers have often defaulted, having been superb at criticizing the old story but offering as an alternative only Western liberal abstractions about humanity.[33] Into the resulting vacuum two alternatives are flowing, the right-wing repetition of the old story in which America is great because she is morally good,[34] and the relentlessly secular legitimation, which holds that America is good because she is technologically great.[35]

By no means will a revisionist legitimation story simply sanctify the status quo! By drawing on the hermeneutic of suspicion as well as the hermeneutic of affirmation, it will not be as blind to the dark side of the American experience as was the old. Native Americans, African Americans, and the descendants of Chinese coolies—to name but a few— will keep us more honest. The new story must incorporate

---

32. For a positive interpretation of basic images and symbols (e.g., Promised Land, Paradise, Covenant, Errand), *see* Richard E. Wentz, *The Saga of the American Soul.* Basic for Wentz is the conviction that the "saga is the bearer of universalizing task" (p. 7); i.e., the American saga embraces all, and simultaneously grounds precisely the criticism of American experience.

33. Robert Wuthnow observes that rarely do liberal religious leaders refer positively to the religious views of the "Founding Fathers" and when they do speak of the nation's role it is in terms not of a special mission but of responsibility. Indeed, "Liberal religious leaders offer little that specifically legitimates America as a nation." In fact, they "may detract from the legitimacy of the current U.S. system rather than contribute to it." Though championing higher principles in the face of the status quo, neither left nor right can claim effectively to speak for consensual values, thereby making religion "sectarian" (*The Restructuring of American Religion,* chap. 11).

34. So Dwight D. Eisenhower, as quoted by Martin Marty, *Religion and Republic,* p. 85.

35. *See* Wuthnow's perceptive observation in *The Restructuring of American Religion,* chap. 11.

the ambiguity of our history and will have both Lincoln's sense of destiny through pain and Niebuhrian irony.[36] It will not be saluted everywhere. In some quarters it will receive a cold stare like the one I once got when, after hearing a park ranger tell the heroic story of Custer's Last Stand, I asked if he had ever told the story from the standpoint of the Indians. The five hundredth anniversary of the arrival of Columbus is a good time to begin thinking about a revisionist story, one that acknowledges our faults but is also not afraid to say, "Nevertheless."

The mainline Protestants have a theological tradition that can guide them here—the doctrine of *simul justus et peccator*. But if they are to participate in the formation of a new story for our people, they must overcome that alienation, guilt, and self-hate that now inhibit their leaders from saying something positive. Then the churches could join with others in putting the genius of the American experiment into better perspective, and thereby be a constructive influence in the competition for the soul of the nation.

The Pitching Coach

Instead of pretending to be the manager, the churches should be the pitching coach, the one who develops the tal-

---

36. Reinhold Niebuhr, *The Irony of American History* (New York: Charles Scribner's Sons, 1952). For an appreciative, yet critical, assessment of Niebuhr, *see* Richard Reinitz, *Irony and Consciousness: American Historiography and Reinhold Niebuhr's Vision*. Reinitz's view of irony is itself Niebuhrian: "We perceive a human action as ironic . . . when we see the consequences of that action as contrary to the original intent of the actor and can locate a significant part of the reason for the discrepancy in the actor himself or in his intention." In such a view of irony, "The contradictory outcome is at least in part a result of an unconscious weakness in ourselves," so that "we are seen as bearing some responsibility for a discrepancy" (p. 19). In contrast with history viewed from the perspective of alienation, Niebuhrian irony entails "at once an acceptance of the humanity of the historical actor and a critical stance toward the consequences of his actions"; "this allows for both empathetic encounter with people of the past that makes historical knowledge possible and the analytic distance that makes them useful" (p. 28). Such an understanding of irony brings to light the vices of human virtues and self-deceptions of goodness.

ents of the players. The deep need for quality leaders is obvious. Even the most progressive legislation will fail if the people who administer it are incompetent, are deficient in character, and lack moral conviction. Do we think that quality leaders can be produced on demand? What institutions and experiences will form their character, shape their vision, and sensitize their consciences to the moral dimensions of life and work? Who will nourish the qualities that make for trustworthy leaders?

The mainline churches, having begun to reach out to minorities and to ordain women, are well positioned to enlarge and develop the talent pool in which strong leaders can be formed. To do so, however, leadership itself must be valued, respected, and rewarded more than it has been recently. I am not equating strong leadership with authoritarianism, but I am interested in changing the attitude in churches and seminaries toward qualities essential for effective leadership. And that means creating an atmosphere in which strong leadership skill is valued, encouraged, and rewarded instead of being denigrated as a remnant of male machismo deserving only exorcism.

Leaders assume responsibility. Consequently, if the churches are to nourish strong leadership they must be more hospitable to persons with strong egos. Some of us can recall when our seminary classmates included a captain of the football or debate team, several student body presidents, the editor of the paper, and others with sufficient ego strength to have already shown their capacities to lead and take responsibility. Today, such persons are more likely to be found in schools of law, business, or medicine than in divinity. The impression is abroad that the church does not welcome strength since it is more a place to find a support group than a channel for energy and talent, more a place where the bruised find solace than where the strong find companions and challenge. I am not longing for a church of Jesus-jocks and wheeler-dealers. The point, rather, is that the churches have the opportunity to nurture the kind of persons that society needs to lead its institutions, including the churches themselves.[37]

It is appropriate that this Beecher lecture conclude by insisting that the preacher be confident that what one says from the pulpit is vital for the development of persons to whom we can entrust the leadership of our institutions. It is the habits of the community of faith, built up week by week, that shape those who lead and those who follow.

To these habits belongs hearing preaching that wrestles with the ambiguities of public affairs; preaching that emphasizes what makes for the common good, especially character marked by integrity, self-control, and respect for all people; preaching that is truly prophetic because it springs more from agony than from alienation; preaching that brings the perspective of eternity to bear on our temporal affairs, whether by revealing the transcendent meaning of the ordinary or by exposing the transient significance of the allegedly momentous; preaching that widens the horizons of love and service because it announces the scope and depth of God's love in Christ; preaching that provokes the pondering of our discipleship and the praising of God's grace. From churches with such habits of hearing, and of the doing that flows from them, can come a cadre of persons who can work effectively for a more just and compassionate society.

The weekly round of preaching and truly pastoral work does not have the reputation of being where the action is,[38]

---

37. Although Susanne Johnson has in view the renewal of Christian spirituality, her observation that "the church is by its very nature a community of formation" is precisely what is in view here (*Christian Spiritual Formation in the Church and Classroom*, p. 28).

38. The Canadian pastor, Philip J. Lee, not only puts in a word on behalf of ordinary Christians and ordinary congregations, but notes that "ecclesiastical bureaucrats often appeal for financial support urging local (ordinary) congregations to spend as much on the greater ministry as they spend on *themselves*, as if money

but in the long run it is where the influence is. What any pluralist society needs from the churches is what only they can give—namely, their vigorous life as authentic and confident communities of faith. It is in such that a new Christian humanism can be envisaged—one that does not settle for affirming the lowest common denominator in a pluralist culture but one that energizes Christians to ennoble whatever space they occupy.[39]

Pastors, take heart! Yours is a great vocation.

---

paying a bureaucrat's salary is holier than money supporting the local pastor. Ordinary congregations also need to be affirmed and encouraged in performing the necessary tasks they have been ordained to do. The Protestant clergy should stand with their congregations in denouncing an elitism that fails to honor the essential work of the ordinary congregation in its own locale" (*Against the Protestant Gnostics*, p. 266).

39. Although the phrase "Christian humanism" appears several times in these pages, the focus of these presentations precludes pursuing the theme here. Several observations must suffice. First, as used here the phrase connotes perspectives that are more culturally oriented than those suggested by the idyllic shalom. Second, because behind the phrase lies the memory of a time when significant elements of our culture—e.g., art, architecture, literature, and music—expressed aspects of the Christian vision of life and death, it tacitly asks whether renewed churches might again stimulate such creativity, thereby freeing the churches from their twentieth-century restriction to politics as the dominant mode of influencing our society. Third, should a new Christian humanism fail to emerge, the churches might well become self-selecting conventicles. The whole matter needs serious rethinking.

CHAPTER FOUR

COMMUNICATION

The mainstream Protestant churches are close to the bottom
ranks of contemporary organizations when it comes to communicating ideas.

> —J. Edward Carothers, *The Paralysis of Mainstream
> Protestant Leadership*

Liberalism has been so busy transforming the Christian tradition that it has forgotten to transmit it.

> —Leonard Sweet, "Can a Mainstream Change Its Course?"

Ages of faith are not marked by "dialogue" but by *proclamation*.

> —Peter Berger, *Facing Up to Modernity*

God is the master of his own revelation; and therefore, he
only succeeds if he wins, not the soul's assent but the soul
itself.

> —P. T. Forsyth, *Positive Preaching and the Modern Mind*

T he self-communication of God is communicated in the gospel. Since the church lives by the gospel, communication is at the heart of its life. Consequently, the renewal of the mainline churches will manifest itself in the renewal of their communication. It is, then, as inevitable as it is appropriate that this penultimate chapter turn to the churches' vocation to communicate.

It is not easy to talk about communication because the word "communication" does not communicate very well; in many minds it conjures up both arcane diagrams with assorted boxes and arrows as well as a jargon that obscures the obvious. Moreover, the subject matter touches virtually everything that animate creatures do—from squawks and gestures to mathematics and artificial intelligence. Likewise, communicating the Christian faith puts everything on the table because no part of human experience is off limits to its influence. Fortunately, the scope of this chapter is much more modest. After noting first the situation in which we find ourselves, we will identify a twofold need in communication—the informative and the imaginative. Then we will turn to the relation of the mainline churches to the gospel.

A New Era

The consequences of the technological advances in communication are so diverse and so deep that they are difficult to grasp and absorb. We are both fascinated and overwhelmed by the relentless change that makes yesterday's wonder today's standard equipment, and today's marvel tomorrow's museum piece. Further, the cumulative impact of these marvels, on the individual as well as on society, is almost beyond comprehension. Those who early saw what was happening and portrayed it in visionary terms, like the late Marshall McLuhan, are now seen as rather premature because they did not foresee the impact of making personal computers and fax machines as common as typewriters once were. In a word, the new electronic marvels are bringing about a change that is systemic, shaping the world in which we literally live and move and have our being. Any renewal of the mainline churches that does not reckon with this change will take them only to the middle of the twentieth century.

Enthusiasts easily claim too much, of course, often suggesting (or perhaps wishing) that everything we have known and valued until now is being swept away. If these be prophets, I am not among them. The new does not displace the old the way a parking meter has replaced a hitching post. Communication in print will continue as an option to be chosen for what it can do best. It will help us to clarify the vocation of the mainliners to communicate if we first look a bit more closely at both modes of communication.

The Second Coming of Technology

At the outset, it is well to recall that the coming of print was to the communication of ideas what the industrial revolution was to the production of goods—namely, standardization. Just as every buyer of a machine-made item uses an identical product, so every reader of a printed book has the identical text. Pierre Babin, Director of the Center for Research and Communication in Lyon, sees the import of such standardization for catechesis, beginning with Luther's Small Catechism of 1529, of which 100,000 copies were sold in forty years. Not only was every reader given identical instruction, but the catechumens were required to memorize it word for word, with no deviation permitted.[1] Comparable developments occurred, he claims, in the post-Tridentine Catholic Church. No wonder that a new mode of

1. Pierre Babin, *The New Era in Religious Communication*, pp. 26-27.

orthodoxy, based on uniformity of language, emerged in Western Christianity generally, as the largely affective and image-oriented faith of the Middle Ages was displaced by a more cerebral form in which precise formulations were essential, and in Protestantism dominant.

The coming of print did not, of course, replace the visual arts, nor did the rationality associated with print eclipse the affective linked with the visual. Rather, they not only co-existed but interacted in multiple ways, as the modern illus-trated book shows. Significant here, however, is discerning the difference between what happens in communication through reading print and communication through seeing images. The ways in which printed words can evoke images is an important subtlety that we can leave aside.

One way of making concrete the difference between the image and the printed word is to consider the ability of each to handle sequence and simultaneity. In reading, as in writ-ing, communication is sequential because whether one reads a sentence, a paragraph, or a poem, one follows the text from beginning to end, as printed. Although the style of a given author might allow the reader to find the key sentence at either the beginning or the end of a paragraph, no one reads a sentence backward. The printed sentence controls the sequence of ideas, especially in English where word order is particularly important. In viewing a painting or a piece of sculpture, however, the communication is simulta-neous as the eye takes in form, line, color, and composition all at once, even if one looks at parts of the work.

The difference becomes even more obvious when one reads a description of a work of art. Then one discovers that the sequence of words and sentences cannot communicate what strikes the eye simultaneously because one can write and read only one thing at a time. In my work as a teacher of the New Testament, repeatedly this phenomenon has frus-trated my efforts to teach the book of Revelation, where a sequence of words tries to convey what sometimes the seer saw simultaneously. In the Apocalypse of John, as in some drama or opera, there are simultaneous actions, which the text must report sequentially. Words like "meanwhile" cannot actually convey what is concurrent but require the reader's mind to overcome the sequence of words by an act of imagination, which usually falls short. In other words, "meanwhile, back at the ranch" never does what a painting would show.

That adding sound to printed words increases their capacity to communicate is obvious, whether one has in view oral reading or singing a libretto. (Parenthetically, this is why a proper public—that is, oral—reading of Scripture is such an important art;[2] far too much reading of Scripture in worship simply dares the Word of the Lord to occur.) What is of interest here, however, is the contrast between what occurs when one reads with eyes and mind, and what happens when the combination of words and sounds is reinforced with visual images; it is one thing to read silently a libretto and score of an opera, another to see and hear it performed. The interaction of staging, costumes, words, and music yields a powerful communication-event. What the silent reader must imagine, the performance presents, affecting the ear, the eye, and the emotions all at once. The Christian church has known this for centuries, of course, for its liturgies are dramatic, stylized celebrations of the faith, not religious programs with commercials for the congregation's activities. In our century, no one understood better how to exploit the capacity of the combination of sound, sight, and words to communicate power than the Nazis, whose rallies at Nuremberg have never been equaled.

2. Walter J. Ong, in discussing the primal connection between the oral and the sacred, observes, "In Christianity, for example, the Bible is read aloud at liturgical services. For God is thought of always as 'speaking' to the human beings, not as writing to them" (*Orality and Literacy*, p. 75).

Today's technology has made it possible for the combination of sound, image, and words to communicate a quite different power. In music video, powerful rhythms and sounds merge with swiftly moving images accompanied by words in order to offer an experience of participation by resonating with the performance. In terms of communicating, the contrast between silent reading and vibrating with MTV could hardly be greater. If reading appeals to reason and reflection, MTV appeals to emotion and immediacy. This mode of communication has been around long enough to have had an impact far beyond sheer entertainment. It has affected what is expected also of religious experience. Indeed, Babin is not off base when he observes that "for many people, faith has acquired a Dionysiac foundation, reliant upon stimulation by drugs, powerful visual and auditory sensations, and video clips" (p. 30).

A New Construal System

It is my purpose not to deliver a moral judgment about this development but to understand its import. As already noted, the technological advances have escalated exponentially the power of those modes of communication for which the printed word is not essential, though on occasion useful. Moreover, TV, video, MTV, and electronic music are of a piece technologically; these media penetrate modern cultures across every political and social barrier, providing entertainment on a scale unprecedented, offering education, propelling economies through advertising, changing lifestyles, and controlling political processes and events. As a result, the phrase "modern communications" refers to nothing less than a coherent, changing construal system.

What is characteristic of this construal system is that it changes the inherited relation of *logos* and *phainomena*, reason and appearances. Instead of appearances and images being perceptible expressions of rational reality, so that images point beyond themselves to intelligible reality, in this construal system technological reason often serves the image by providing the rationale and the know-how for manipulating images for the desired emotion-driven effects. For example, when the churches relied on the traditional construal system, they used audio-visual aids to assist the communication of ideas. But in the new system the auditory and the visual materials are not aids; they blend with the subject matter itself in order to evoke an experience. If television provides us with "a worldview which not only determines what we think, but also how we think and who we are," as William Fore contends,[3] how much more true is it of the systemic whole! Because the reality to which we relate is the image, the image we project becomes the reality we are. In this light, we understand Babin's dictum, "'Being seen' is being" (p. 46).

Occasionally, print-oriented people are accused of not absorbing what has happened in communication. (Indeed, giving a lecture on the subject is itself an ironic event.) But the accusation is partly misplaced because this inversion of *logos* and *phainomena* can no more be absorbed into the inherited view than the 12-tone musical system can be absorbed into the traditional octave. Instead, it must be recognized for what it is—a systemic alternative, whose impact on our sensibility, on our ways of perceiving, organizing, and construing reality is comparable with the way Romanticism challenged the Enlightenment.

As noted in passing, this technologically birthed construal system will not sweep away the print-oriented one but will continue alongside it, and challenge it on various levels. I see no adequate basis for wishing that it would replace the tradi-

---

3. William F. Fore, *Television and Religion: The Shaping of Faith, Values, and Culture*, p. 22.

tion, as if the new brought the Kingdom. Nor do I see any reason to demonize it and the communications industry wholesale. Rather, the mainline churches' vocation calls for understanding it as clearly, as comprehensively, as penetratingly as possible, in order to learn what both image-dominated media and the printed word can and cannot communicate well.

The Vocation to Communicate

Because there is a communicative aspect to everything that we do, it is necessary to make some distinctions before we proceed farther. In this context, it is convenient to distinguish communication to insiders, the transmission of the Christian tradition within the churches, from communication to outsiders. Clearly, this is a somewhat arbitrary distinction, for some within the family of faith are outside the institutional church and vice versa. The distinction is useful nonetheless because it allows focusing here on the vocation of the mainline churches to communicate the Christian faith and tradition to that part of our secularized pluralist society not involved with the churches. It is therefore important to distinguish three aspects of this vocation; they will be identified as we proceed.

Informing the Pluralist Public

If the mainline churches are half as serious about the well-being of our society as they frequently claim, they will double their efforts to interpret the Christian tradition to those beyond their orbits; this is because pluralism is healthy only if everyone is present and voting, if there are no absentee ballots, if each group is unequivocal about the commitments and habits that shape its identity. Healthy pluralism cannot be taken for granted but requires maintenance. To this

maintenance the mainliners can contribute when they interpret the Christian tradition unabashedly to others so that
they can understand what they do not accept.[4] Central to
such self-interpretation is information about the faith and its
traditions. Purveying information is, of course, the basic
form of communication, and the most effective medium for
doing so remains print-oriented, partly because it can be
clear and partly because it appeals to the mind. In fulfilling
this responsibility of informing the public, the mainliners
should forge a new apologetics.

Apologetics has had an interesting career, beginning with
the second-century Christians, who learned the art from
Hellenized Jews. Both relied on written apologies to state
their cases in categories that the Greco-Roman world could
understand readily; these apologies were designed to dimin-
ish hostility resulting from sheer misunderstanding as well as
from the suspicions of the state. In modern times, Protestant
orthodoxy developed a rationalist apologetics as a subfield of
theology in order to defend the truth of Christian doctrine
against unbelief. Liberal Protestantism, however, moved in
another direction. Instead of defending the castle against the
onslaught of modern unbelief, it followed Schleiermacher's
policy and negotiated a series of cease-fires with modernity
in order to salvage the gold and silver by abandoning the
rest. What was rescued was recast into thought patterns

---

4. I am pleased to discover that what is proposed here agrees with Winthrop
Hudson's analysis of late-nineteenth-century Protestantism: "The deeper malady
was the theological erosion which had taken place. . . . A pluralistic society is a
highly competitive society—a society in which various traditions are locked into
debate. In such a situation, presuppositions must be clearly defined and their implications carefully articulated, if a particular religious group is to survive and make its
influence felt. This means that the adherents of the several traditions must be
knowledgeable and informed. They must be able to spell out its implications with
clarity and persuasiveness. Otherwise they are not equipped to participate effectively in the discussion. It is precisely at this point that American Protestantism had
become weak" (Quoted from *American Protestantism*, in Wilson and Drakeman,
Church and State in American History, p. 149).

deemed acceptable to the modern mind—often with the claim that the paraphrase had been the real meaning all along. Thus liberal Protestant theology itself became apologetics, this time oriented as much to the church as to the world, whose "cultured despisers" it rather admired. Although Barth repudiated such compacts, the negotiations have resumed, though by now two things have become clear: There seems to be less and less left to salvage, and the terms proposed by the church negotiators are of interest mostly to themselves.[5]

Perhaps what is envisioned here ought not to be called apologetics at all, for its intent is neither to dispel opposition, nor to make the Christian faith acceptable to that elusive thing called "the modern (or postmodern) mind"; its aim, rather, is to present the Christian faith and its tradition as an intelligible and plausible construal of reality.[6] Because its

---

5. George A. Lindbeck's observation is beyond dispute: "Liberal attempts to explain religions by translating them into other conceptualities seem to appeal chiefly to theologians or to other religious people" (*Nature of Doctrine,* p. 129).

6. The extent to which "apologetics" is the right word depends on whether one regards it as a form of catechesis—instruction in the faith for serious inquirers and prospective adherents—or as pre-catechetical, as understood here. This difference accounts for the divergence of this proposal from that in George Lindbeck's important book, *The Nature of Doctrine.* My proposal agrees with Lindbeck at important points: (a) that religions can be understood as "comprehensive interpretive schemes," which, like a language, shape the subjectivities of the individual (and community) instead of being primarily a manifestation of them, as liberal Protestantism held (p. 33); (b) that Christianity cannot be translated into something else in order to make it credible, because religions "can no more be taught by means of translation [i.e., "taught" as imparted] than Chinese or French" (p. 29); (c) that therefore the Christian faith must be taught within the church as a coherent whole, not as an ad-hoc jerry-built aggregate of sundry beliefs. Because Lindbeck aims to overcome precisely the collapse of theology into apologetics, which marked liberal Protestantism since Schleiermacher, he sees little place for apologetics-as-catechesis in a pluralist culture.

I, on the other hand, propose that a pre-catechetical apologetics designed to inform rather than to impart or convert has a vital role precisely in an authentically pluralist culture. An informative apologetic might well lead to catechesis for some, but such an outcome must not distort the informative nature of the task as envisioned here. Jews, for instance, have often suspected that many a "dialogue" is really a smoke-screen for conversion.

intent is to inform and interpret rather than to defend and persuade, it would use the hermeneutic of suspicion in order to tell it like it is and was, and so avoid presenting a doctored self-portrait; it would also use the hermeneutic of affirmation to allow the plausibility of the classical Christian faith to emerge clearly.

Undertaking such an informational apologetic will require the mainline churches, like all churches, to overcome what they have mastered—the art of talking to themselves. Christianity is awash in publications. More than any other religion, Christianity has baptized the printing press and its current technological marvels. Never before has so much productivity been sent to print. Enormous amounts of money and creativity are committed to producing curriculum resources, Bible commentaries and dictionaries on every level of sophistication, books and tapes dealing with everything from spirituality to church administration, and most of it designed for internal consumption. (The general level of knowledge about the Christian faith *within* the churches suggests that these publications have not been notably effective.)[7] Every denomination has its house organ to report sundry activities of interest only to its own members. Advocacy journals like *The Christian Century, Christianity Today,* or *Sojourners* tend to reinforce the mindset of their like-minded readership. Publications like the *Journal of Biblical Literature, Church History,* or the *Journal for the Study of the Pseudepigrapha* are produced for fellow professionals and are too technical to be intelligible to the amateur, and often to other professionals as well. On the whole, there simply is very little publication that informs the general nonchurch reader about Christianity the way *Scientific American* or *Smithsonian* informs the wider public about

---

7. Despite the generally above-average level of education in the "mainline" churches, one has the impression that often the more liberal, the less literate in the Christian tradition.

various aspects of our culture—in a readable, nontechnical way that is reliable, perceptive, and interesting.

But where is the cadre of Christian communicators who can write informatively and engagingly about Christianity the way Carl Sagan does about astronomy? The mainline churches do not even notice that something important is missing. As a result, what the nonchurch public knows about Christianity is an odd assortment of skewed childhood memories of Sunday School or parochial school (and more and more, there is less and less of this to recall), and what is picked up from the steadily reduced number of pieces in popular magazines[8] or from the evening news on television. In the public press, religion is quarantined in the church page (or quarter page if one subtracts the church ads)—unless there is a papal visit, a denominational fight, or a sex scandal involving a televangelist.

The massive ignorance about Christianity will not abate unless the churches begin to assume some responsibility for informing the public about themselves and their faith. The same is true of seminaries, for they are not noted for their passion to identify, encourage, and train persons who can communicate engagingly with the nonchurch world. To be sure, preaching courses discourage sermons that use only in-group language, but most sermons are designed for persons already in church. Few mainline seminaries, if any, offer courses in preaching to the so-called unchurched, and fewer still train writers to communicate with the general public.

---

8. The evidence gathered by Dennis N. Voskull shows that whereas *Time* and *Newsweek* once included a "Religion" section each week, by the 1970s they often went three or four weeks without paying any attention to religion at all. Moreover, before the 60s nearly half of all the stories about religion were related to one of the mainline churches, and a bulk of the remainder to the Catholic Church; in the 50s, six Protestant leaders were on the cover of *Time*. Since then, the visibility of mainline Protestantism has been replaced by that accorded to various conservative and charismatic groups ("Reaching Out: Mainline Protestantism and the Media," in Hutchison, *Between the Times,* pp. 77-80).

Neither the churches nor the divinity schools will find their vocation to communicate effectively to the general public so long as they are spooked by the charge that concern for thorough and accurate knowledge, clear thinking, concise expression, and thoughtful use of the English language are the marks of an elitism that must go. But since when are shoddy thinking and incompetent use of our language hallmarks of a true church or gifts of the Spirit? The matter is urgent, for unless mainline churches are able to communicate to the wider public who they are, what they believe, and what difference that can make; unless they are able to communicate the character and content of the Christian tradition, they will become an endangered species of interest mostly to their professional caste and historians.

We do not have to invent the wheel. There is a rich heritage of rhetoric waiting to be tapped—rhetoric that is not adornment but the art of communicating effectively. There is also a vast body of resources in the modern field of communication, which, though often jargon-filled and trendy (rather like theology), can be explored and appropriated with profit. There are also things to be learned from precedents like the efforts by the Anti-Defamation League on behalf of the Jewish tradition.

Cultivating a Positive Disposition

The mainline churches' vocation in communication has also a second aspect—cultivating a disposition, a readiness, to hear and perhaps heed the gospel. Although this aspect also relies on information, its aim is different enough to call for somewhat different skills. Whereas the informational task finds print-shaped communication more appropriate, this preparatory task will find the electronic media which combine the visual and the auditory useful because they touch the affective and the volitional aspects of the self more directly than print.

Responding to this need also requires a changed attitude, for it is no secret that the mainline churches have not known what to do with television. At first, they relied on their quasi-establishment status to get free public service time. But then they were crowded off the air by entrepreneurial figures who bought their time by asking the viewers to pay for it. (Apparently only the Seventh Day Adventist Church has paid for its broadcast time.) By 1977, the peak year of religious broadcasting,[9] paid-time religious broadcasts accounted for 92 percent of the total of religious programming.[10] Unfortunately, the conservative and fundamentalist users of TV regard it simply as a marvelous tool to spread the gospel, being quite oblivious of the impact of the medium on the message. Peter Horsfield observes,

> Paid time religious programs are perhaps the finest example of sophisticated, market-researched consumer faith. Rightly perceiving the nature of the television environment and having to succeed financially in it, the broadcasters have allowed their programs to be almost totally shaped by it. By making themselves financially dependent on this environment and its inhabitants, they have removed their capacity to change it.[11]

The common criticisms of religious TV need not be repeated here. More germane is the criticism that can be leveled at the mainline churches who complain about TV evangelism but offer no alternative but their own talking heads. Indeed, Fore claims that what religious TV has

---

9. Peter G. Horsfield, *Religious Television,* p. 107.

10. Ibid., p. 89.

11. Ibid., pp. 46, 53; *see also* William F. Fore, *Television and Religion,* p. 53.

revealed is the enormous human hurt, loneliness, and meaninglessness among our people and which the mainliners have
largely ignored.[12] Although these churches view themselves
as compassionate caregivers, many followers of religious TV
see the churches as being quite indifferent to the needs and
hurts of ordinary people. Whatever be the cause of this failure in communication, the main point is that the churches,
being mostly incompetent bystanders, have little moral
ground for trashing the misusers of television. Late in the
day it may be, but it is not too late for the mainliners to do
something positive in communicating through TV.

To begin with, television should not be feared, avoided,
or, in the name of being prophetic, damned as the electronic Anti-Christ. Like most things, TV has its good as
well as its bad side. So it must first of all be understood, by
which I mean not its machinery but its inner, driving logic.
One thing that emerged from Yale Divinity School's recent
brief experimentation with communication is the conviction that the future leadership of the mainline churches
needs to know enough about the TV industry to dispel the
mystery and the mythology with which it is now endowed.
One cannot relate constructively to what is not understood, and this includes understanding it from the inside
as well as from the outside as a construal system. In recent
decades, theological schools have developed impressive
field placements with hospitals, counseling centers, shel-
ters for the homeless and abused, as well as prisons. I see
no good reason why they should not do the same with an
institution and an industry whose influence on the mindset
and values of our society is without parallel. Has fear pre-
vented such a development—fear of being associated with
televangelism on the one hand, and of being tainted by
laboring in the devil's own shop on the other? In any case,

---

12. Fore, *Television and Religion*, p. 100.

this avoidance is comparable to liberal Protestantism's aversion to chaplaincies in the armed services, the flip side of which is the passion to be morally pure and politically correct.

In the second place, the mainline churches should not abandon the people in the television industry. Many of them are more aware of its problems than we are, and welcome having someone in the churches who understands what they face daily. When the Divinity School began to explore the area of communication a few years ago, we made contact with journalists, publishers, and broadcasters first of all to listen. In every case we were welcomed, sometimes with amazement because we did not presume to tell them what they should be doing. A ministry to the people in the industry too is important.

Third, the mainliners should begin to experiment with programming that is consonant with the peculiar nature of TV—its capacity to motivate by being immediate and intimate. But given the enormous costs, of energy as well as of money, programming should be limited to the occasional which can be done well. Being experienced ecumenists, they can sponsor jointly programs that suggest, invite, and lure the reader toward the rich resources of the Christian tradition without openly advocating them. For such programming, the arts—both visual and musical—would be especially important. Those who have seen Bill Moyers' program "Amazing Grace," or have heard Kathleen Battle and Jessye Norman sing spirituals without chattering about them, know what I mean. Music— whether Sacred Harp, the religious repertoire of country music, the liturgies of the ethnic churches or of the Orthodox tradition—is a marvelous resource for making the cultural distillations of the Christian faith accessible to those who either have never known them or would welcome being reminded of them. Much the same could be said of the visual arts, and carefully crafted drama, once it is clear that the aim is to communicate something of the faith to which each viewer can relate on his or her own terms, and not to persuade the critics that Christians too can be sophisticated.

No less important are programs about ordinary people's efforts to be faithful Christians. Let others parade the testimonies of the rich and famous. The ordinary folk, the uncelebrated Christians doing remarkable things, and occasionally failing, often make far more interesting and convincing programs than the hagiography of the successful. Exactly the same is true of congregations as well.

To pursue these possibilities concretely, the churches need to absorb what various lines of research have shown— that the televangelists are wrong when they insist that TV is an effective tool for evangelism. Televangelism's main effect is to reinforce the religious views and commitments the audience already has. There is nothing wrong with that, of course. But reinforcement is one thing, evangelism another. Despite a certain amount of anecdotal evidence, network TV can never be a truly proper means of evangelism because it cannot connect people with a real community of faith, a local church. What this medium can do best is what I have been talking about—arouse curiosity about and cultivate a positive disposition toward Christianity.[13]

Using television, as well as videotapes, requires the churches to take some risks by entrusting the task to a cadre of competent persons who understand that the aim is not to convince but to arouse interest and evoke significant questions. There are such persons, often far more eager to use their talents in this way than the churches have been to enlist them.

---

13. *See also* Fore, *Television and Religion*, pp. 51, 122; Horsfield, *Religious Television*, p. 175.

Commending the Gospel Confidently

There is little point in arousing interest in the Christian faith if the mainline churches lack sufficient conviction to commend the gospel with confidence and compassion.

A century and more ago, the word "evangelical" had not yet been appropriated by a cluster of churches or a caucus within them but would have been used by virtually all Protestants, for they were committed to evangelizing their fellow Americans and the so-called heathen abroad. But that was before the tragic hiatus between those committed to the Social Gospel and those committed to saving souls—a split which resulted in what Martin Marty has called the Two Party System.[14] The fundamentalist-modernist battles only deepened the mutual alienation. To be sure, the mainliners have not repudiated evangelism; they simply put it on the back burner where it could be kept warm enough to mollify those elements among them which continue to value it highly. To shift metaphors, the fires of evangelistic commitment have been banked for the duration.[15]

The great strength of the mainline churches, guided by the liberal apologetic stemming from Schleiermacher, has

---

14. Martin E. Marty, *Righteous Empire*, 1970; 2nd ed., published as *Protestantism in the United States*, chap. 19.

15. On the world scene, the mainliners have steadily reduced their overseas missionary staffs—partly in response to the demand, "Missionary, go home!" and partly in order to allow indigenous churches to grow on their own terms. Meanwhile, conservative and fundamentalist churches, as well as independent evangelists, have expanded their own overseas work dramatically, so that today there are more American missionaries overseas than ever before. According to David Barrett, the well-known statistician of world Christianity, in 1900 there were 62,000 foreign missionaries from all countries, and in 1992 there were 295,000, most of them Americans (*International Bulletin of Missionary Research* 16 [January 1992]: 27). He also reports that a wide assortment of plans, in fifty languages, have been generated to evangelize the world by the year 2000. The mainliners, however, continue to regard conversion as quite secondary to service, partly because they have become uncertain about the relation of Christianity to other religions. This is indeed a pressing issue of our time, but it cannot be discussed here.

been their ability to help individuals be modern persons and Christians at the same time—if they insisted on it.

Many of us have benefited from these efforts and have participated in them as well. At the same time, this pattern has also yielded two unforeseen consequences: On the one hand, by making the substance of the faith continually more palatable to the increasingly secular mind, the hearty gumbo of the Christian faith has been thinned so often that there is little nourishment left. On the other hand, by concentrating on how one *can* be a Christian and a modern person at the same time something vital has been lost: the conviction that one *ought to be* a Christian. Unless the mainline recovers its confidence in the gospel enough to commend it heartily, the future of these churches will be bleak indeed.

Recovering such confidence in the gospel requires two things: Needed first is the conviction that the gospel is true enough that believing it makes a decisive difference at the center of one's life, whether or not the observation is accurate that "the typical American is a Calvinist who has neither fear of hell nor hope of heaven."[16]

Also needed is a deep love and compassion for persons whose lives are in disarray because they do not or cannot yet rely on their Creator, are not yet rightly related to their God. If the character and condition of a person's relation to God is primary because this determines who one is and how one is in the world, then lowering suffering and raising consciousness—important as they may be—are not enough to set right the self at its center. If Jesus was right in saying that it is not what goes into a person's mouth that defiles one but what comes out of the heart, then the human heart's relation to its Creator deserves more attention from the mainliners than it has received even through pastoral care. Historian Edwin Gaustad is on the mark in observing, "The fault of much

---

16. Norman Birnbaum, as quoted by Marty, *Religion and Republic*, p. 127.

pietism is that it sought to save souls apart from the world. The fault of much of liberalism is that it sought to save the world apart from the soul. In recent years, the 'new evangelicals' have done more to redress their imbalance than have the 'old liberals.'"[17] What many people miss in the mainline churches is a concern for the well-being of their personal— not private—relation to God, for the health of their souls.

To insist on recovering these things—the conviction that the gospel matters, and a passionate concern for a person's relation to God—is nothing other than to summon the mainline churches to reclaim what is already theirs, in their own heritage, and to reclaim it not as one accepts an heirloom that is dusted but left unused, but as an inheritance whose rediscovery renews the whole household. If that happens, these churches can once more commend the gospel with confidence. And hungering and distraught people will hear again some Good News from their pulpits. And then the grim-faced Christianity of today's liberal Protestantism will discover that it can laugh again, and perhaps break out in the praise of God.

---

17. Edwin S. Gaustad, "Our Country: One Century Later," in Michaelson and Roof, *Liberal Protestantism*, p. 101.

RETROSPECTIVE REMARKS
ABOUT RENEWAL

I t is useful to look back at the terrain covered. The fore-going chapters have asserted that renewal will be insep-arable from the worshipful praise of God; that it will entail a rebirth of serious theology grounded in the classical Christian tradition, affirmed critically; that renewal will require a new vision of what it means to be faithful in a pluralist culture without retreating into a religious ghetto; and that recovering the vocation to communicate is an essential hallmark of the renewal. All four changes are necessary if the mainline churches are to enter the next century with confidence.

Clearly, many aspects of the four topics did not surface in these chapters, and a number of other topics, also important for the theme of renewal, could not be accommodated within the framework of four lectures, now committed to print. This is not the place to make up for these omissions. It is appropriate, however, to note briefly some of these topics, each of which was, in fact, a candidate for inclusion but was set aside for reasons that need not be ventilated here.

Among them is that essential, yet amorphous, factor commonly labeled "spirituality." Given the basically personal character of spiritual discipline and devotion, even when nurtured in groups within the congregation (often another item on the list of parish "activities"!), consideration of this topic should focus on developing the spirituality of the whole congregation—*without* fostering a voluble elitism or frightening off those who insist that *their* spirituality is expressed in the community soup kitchen. If a new Christian sensibility is indeed aborning it will combine disciplined personal piety and varied participation in public affairs, including service.

Another topic meriting inclusion in a fuller treatment of the theme concerns the reverse flow of influence on the mainliners from the churches that resulted from their own missionary efforts. As their offspring mature and so increasingly find their own voices, their confident vitality might well become a factor in the renewal of the mainline churches. Such influence from abroad would probably be of a somewhat different sort from that of liberation theology, which has been welcomed mostly by the "new class."

A third topic that deserves attention is the role of theological education in mainline renewal—and vice versa. Although the diverse relationships between the churches and the seminaries and divinity schools (even within a given denomination), make considering this topic exceedingly complex, it is becoming apparent that far too often the seminaries' current turn toward the churches has been motivated more by tribal and financial considerations than by vocational ones. Seminaries too have distinct vocations, which are easily dissipated by burgeoning programs. A healthy relationship between church and school is characterized by a dialectic, as subtle as it is supple, of commitment and criticism. Just as seminaries will not prosper with closer supervision by unrenewed churches, so the renewal of the churches will not be advanced by seminaries in which theological scholarship either ignores the needs of the churches or becomes so preoccupied with the churches that it merely retails basic research done elsewhere.

Although the focus here has been on those intramural matters for which the churches are responsible, their future will also reflect their responses to external factors that they can neither shape nor control, such as the health of our global economy and the ecological crisis. Most important, the worldwide setting of the churches' faith and work has been changed decisively by the collapse of the Soviet Union and the discrediting of Communism on which it was based— concurrent, ironically, with the exposure of our system's inability to sustain its capacity to provide a decent life for millions. For virtually the entire century, the churches have had to deal with a world plagued by multiple ideological polarizations, the consequences of which will become visible relentlessly. Now a new era is dawning. If in this yet ill-defined era the churches are renewed within because they recover their confidence in the gospel, they will be able to offer the twenty-first century a vital witness to the truth about God—and about ourselves.

Perhaps it is not too much to hope that in the closing years of this wretched century, in which human ingenuity managed not only to turn technological marvels into unprecedented horrors but to legitimate the decimation of millions, we will see the beginnings of a sobered view of the human condition. The mainline churches, by contributing the wisdom of their heritage to such a rethinking, might desist from sanctifying utopian illusions and, instead, forge a vision of a new Christian humanism for Adam east of Eden.

What is important to remember however, is this: We could bring to pass everything that has been considered, and more, and still not find the churches renewed. And for that we should be profoundly grateful, because were it not so, the renewal of the churches would not be in God's hands but in ours.

Fortunately, the alternatives cannot be reduced to either renewed churches or churches renewed according to the stratagems of professors and professional Christians operating without the blessing of God. There is no reason to think that God will renew the churches without any human instrument, even if the Lord need not respect our nominations for the task. If divine providence wills the renewal of the mainline churches, it will find the right instruments for it. And should this happen, I trust that the rest of us will have the wisdom and the grace to greet it gladly and thereby be renewed ourselves.

WORKS CITED

Ahlstrom, Sydney. *A Religious History of the American People.* New Haven: Yale University Press, 1972.

Babin, Pierre. *The New Era in Religious Communication.* Minneapolis: Fortress Press, 1991.

Barrett, David B. "Annual Statistical Table on Global Mission: 1900." *International Bulletin of Missionary Research* 16 (January 1992): 26-27.

Bass, Dorothy C. "Ministry on the Margin: Protestants and Education." In Hutchison, *Between the Times,* pp. 48-71.

Bellah, Robert N. *The Broken Covenant: American Civil Religion in Time of Trial.* New York: Seabury Press, 1975.

Berger, Peter L. "American Religion: Conservative Upsurge, Liberal Prospects." In Michaelson and Roof, eds., *Liberal Protestantism,* pp. 19-36.

———. "Different Gospels: The Social Sources of Apostasy." In Neuhaus, *American Apostasy: The Triumph of "Other" Gospels,* pp. 1-14.

Berger, Peter L. *Facing Up to Modernity: Excursions in Society, Politics, and Religion.* New York: Basic Books, 1977.

Braaten, Carl E., *Justification: The Article by Which the Church Stands or Falls.* Minneapolis: Fortress Press, 1990.

Braaten, Carl E. "The Problem of God-Language Today." In *Our Naming of God: Problem and Prospects of God-Talk Today.* Minneapolis: Fortress Press, 1989, chap. 1.

Brueggemann, Walter. *Israel's Praise: Doxology Against Idolatry and Ideology.* Philadelphia: Fortress Press, 1988.

Carothers, J. Edward. *The Paralysis of Mainstream Protestant Leadership.* Nashville: Abingdon Press, 1990.

Clebsch, William A. *From Sacred to Profane America: The Role of Reli-*

gion in American History. Chico, Calif.: Scholars Press, n.d.; orig. published by Harper & Row, 1968.

Dumitriu, Petru. *To the Unknown God.* Trans. James Kirkup. London: Collins, 1982.

Dyrness, William A. *How Does America Hear the Gospel?* Grand Rapids: Wm. B. Eerdmans Publishing Co., 1989.

Edwards, David L. *Christian England.* III: *From the Eighteenth Century to the First World War.* London: Collins, 1984.

———. *The Futures of Christianity.* London: Hodder & Stoughton, 1987.

Emswiler, Thomas N., and Sharon N. Emswiler. *Wholeness in Worship.* San Francisco: Harper & Row, 1980.

Fackre, Gabriel. "Reorientation and Retrieval in Systematic Theology." *The Christian Century* 108, no. 20 (June 26–July 3, 1991): 653-56.

Feuer, Lewis S. *Ideology and the Ideologists.* New York: Harper & Row, 1975.

Fore, William F. *Television and Religion: The Shaping of Faith, Values, and Culture.* Minneapolis: Augsburg Publishing House, 1987.

Forsyth, P. T. *Positive Preaching and the Modern Mind* (Lyman Beecher Lectures, 1906–1907). London: Hodder & Stoughton, 1907; 3rd. ed: Independent Press, 1949.

Frei, Hans W., *The Eclipse of Biblical Narrative: A Study in Enlightenment and Nineteenth-century Hermeneutics.* New York and London: Yale University Press, 1974.

Gaustad, Edwin S. "Our Country: One Century Later." In Michaelson and Roof, eds., *Liberal Protestantism*, pp. 85-101.

Gilbert, Alan D. *The Making of Post-Christian Britain: A History of the Secularization of Modern Society.* London and New York: Longman, 1980.

Hauerwas, Stanley. "Discipleship as a Craft, Church as Disciplined Community." *The Christian Century* 108, no. 27 (October 2, 1991): 881-84.

Hauerwas, Stanley, and William H. Willimon. *Resident Aliens: A Provocative Christian Assessment of Culture and Ministry for People Who Know That Something Is Wrong.* Nashville: Abingdon Press, 1989.

Holmer, Paul L. *The Grammar of Faith.* San Francisco: Harper & Row, 1978.

Horsfield, Peter G. *Religious Television: The Experience in America.* New York and London: Longman, 1984.

Hutchison, William R., ed. *Between the Times: The Travail of the Protestant Establishment in America, 1900–1960.* Cambridge: Cambridge University Press, 1989.

Jensen, Robert W. "A 'Protestant Constructive Response' to Christian Unbelief." In Neuhaus, *American Apostasy,* pp. 56-74.

Jewett, Robert. *The Captain America Complex: The Dilemma of Zealous Nationalism.* Philadelphia: Westminster Press, 1973.

Johnson, Paul. "The Almost-Chosen People: Why America Is Different." In Neuhaus, *Unsecular America,* pp. 1-13.

Johnson, Paul. *Intellectuals.* New York: Harper & Row, 1988; Perennial Library ed., 1990.

Johnson, Susanne. *Christian Spiritual Formation in the Church and Classroom.* Nashville: Abingdon Press, 1989.

Käsemann, Ernst. *The Testament of Jesus: A Study of the Gospel of John in the Light of Chapter 17.* Philadelphia: Fortress Press, 1968.

Kaufman, Gordon D. *An Essay on Theological Method.* AAR Studies in Religion II. Missoula, Mont.: Scholars Press, 1979. Rev. ed.

———. *God the Problem.* Cambridge: Harvard University Press, 1972.

———. *The Theological Imagination: Constructing the Concept of God.* Philadelphia: Westminster Press, 1981.

Kavanagh, Aidan. *On Liturgical Theology.* New York: Pueblo Publishing Co., 1984.

Ladd, Everett Carll. "Secular and Religious America." In Neuhaus, *Unsecular America,* pp. 14-30.

Lee, Philip J. *Against the Protestant Gnostics.* New York and Oxford: Oxford University Press, 1987.

Liechty, Daniel. *Theology in Postliberal Perspective.* Philadelphia: Trinity Press International; London: SCM Press, 1990.

Lindbeck, George A. *The Nature of Doctrine: Religion and Theology in a Postliberal Age.* Philadelphia: Westminster Press, 1984.

Mabee, Charles. *Reimaging America: A Theological Critique of the American Metaphor and Biblical Hermeneutics.* Macon, Ga.: Mercer University Press, 1985.

McBrien, Richard P. *Caesar's Coin: Religion and Politics in America.* New York: Macmillan; London: Collier Macmillan Books, 1987.

McFague, Sallie. *Metaphorical Theology: Models of God in Religious Language.* Philadelphia: Fortress Press, 1982.

Machen, J. Gresham. *Christianity and Liberalism.* Grand Rapids: Wm. B. Eerdmans Publishing Co., n.d. (orig. published 1923).

Marsden, George M. "Are Secularists the Threat? Is Religion the Solution?" In Neuhaus, *Unsecular America,* pp. 31-51.

Marty, Martin E. *Protestantism in the United States: Righteous Empire.* New York: Charles Scribner's Sons. London: Collier Macmillan, 1986 (rev. ed. of *Righteous Empire,* 1970).

———. *The Public Church: Mainline—Evangelical—Catholic.* New York: Crossroad, 1981.

———. *Religion and Republic: The American Circumstance.* Boston: Beacon Press, 1987.

Michaelson, Robert, and Wade Clark Roof, eds. *Liberal Protestantism: Realities and Possibilities.* New York: Pilgrim Press, 1986.

Micks, Marianne H. *The Future Present: The Phenomenon of Christian Worship.* New York: Seabury Press, 1970.

Miller, Patrick D., Jr. "Enthroned on the Praises of Israel." *Interpretation* 39 (1985): 5-19.

Moltmann, Jürgen. *The Church in the Power of the Spirit.* San Francisco: HarperCollins, 1991 (orig. published 1977).

Moore, R. Laurence. *Religious Outsiders and the Making of Americans.* New York and Oxford: Oxford University Press, 1986.

Morrison, Charles Clayton. *What Is Christianity?* (Lyman Beecher Lectures, 1939). Chicago and New York: Willett, Clark and Co., 1940.

Neuhaus, Richard John. *The Catholic Moment: The Paradox of the Church in the Postmodern Age.* San Francisco: Harper & Row, 1987.

Neuhaus, Richard John, ed. *American Apostasy: The Triumph of "Other" Gospels.* Grand Rapids: Wm. B. Eerdmans Publishing Co., 1989.

———, ed. *Unsecular America.* Grand Rapids: Wm. B. Eerdmans Publishing Co., 1986.

Neusner, Jacob, William S. Green, and Ernest Frerichs. *Judaisms and Their Messiahs at the Turn of the Christian Era.* Cambridge: Cambridge University Press, 1987.

Newman, David R. *Worship as Praise and Empowerment.* New York: Pilgrim Press, 1988.

Niebuhr, H. Richard. *Faith on Earth: An Inquiry into the Structure of Human Faith.* New Haven: Yale University Press, 1989.

Niebuhr, Reinhold. *Pious and Secular America.* New York: Charles Scribner and Sons, 1958.

Noll, Mark A. *One Nation Under God? Christian Faith and Political Action in America.* San Francisco: Harper & Row, 1988.

Noll, Mark A., Nathan O. Hatch, and George M. Marsden. *The Search for Christian America.* Westchester, Ill.: Crossway Books, 1983.

Oden, Thomas C. *After Modernity . . . What? Agenda for Theology.* Grand Rapids: Zondervan, 1990.

Ong, Walter J. *Orality and Literacy: The Technologizing of the Word.* London and New York: Methuen, 1982.

Pelikan, Jaroslav. *The Vindication of Tradition.* The 1983 Jefferson Lecture in the Humanities. New Haven and London: Yale University Press, 1984.

Procter-Smith, Marjorie. *In Her Own Rite: Constructing Feminist Liturgical Tradition.* Nashville: Abingdon Press, 1990.

Ramsey, Paul. *Who Speaks for the Church? A Critique of the 1966 Geneva Conference on Church and Society.* Nashville/New York: Abingdon Press, 1967.

Raschke, Carl A. "The Deconstruction of God." In T. J. J. Altizer, et al., *Deconstruction and Theology.* New York: Crossroad, 1982, pp. 1-33.

Reinitz, Richard. *Irony and Consciousness: American Historiography and Reinhold Niebuhr's Vision.* Lewisburg, Pa.: Bucknell University Press; London and Toronto: Associated University Presses, 1980.

Robinson, John A. T. *The New Reformation?* London: SCM Press, 1965.

Rochelle, Jay C. "Doxology and Trinity." In Braaten, *Our Naming of God,* pp. 127-43.

Roof, Wade Clark, and William McKinney. *American Mainline Religion: Its Changing Shape and Future.* New Brunswick and London: Rutgers University Press, 1987.

Ruskin, John. "The Laws of Fésole," *The Works of John Ruskin,* E. T. Cook and Alexander Wedderburn, eds. London: George Allen; New York: Longmans, Green & Co., 1904, vol. 14, pp. 352-53.

Schneider, Robert A. "Voice of Many Waters: Church Federation in the Twentieth Century." In Hutchison, *Between the Times,* pp. 95-121.

Soskice, Janet Martin. *Metaphor and Religious Language.* Oxford: Clarendon Press, 1985.

Sweet, Leonard. "Can a Mainstream Change Its Course?" In Michaelson and Roof, *Liberal Protestantism,* pp. 235-62.

———. "The Modernization of Protestant Religion in America." In *Altered Landscapes: Christianity in America,* 1935–85 (R. Handy Festschrift), D. Lotz, D. Shiver, and J. Wilson, eds. Grand Rapids: Wm. B. Eerdmans Publishing Co., 1989, pp. 19-41.

Voskuil, Dennis N. "Reaching Out: Protestantism and the Media." In Hutchison, *Between the Times,* pp. 72-92.

Wainwright, Geoffrey. "The Praise of God in the Theological Reflection of the Church." *Interpretation* 39 (1985): 34-45.

Wallace, Mark I. *The Second Naivete: Barth, Ricoeur, and the New Yale Theology.* Studies in American Biblical Hermeneutics 6. Macon, Ga.: Mercer University Press, 1990.

Wentz, Richard E. *The Saga of the American Soul.* Washington, D.C.: University Press of America, 1980.

Wilson, John F., and Donald L. Drakeman, eds. *Church and State in American History: The Burden of Religious Pluralism.* Boston: Beacon Press, 1987; second, expanded edition.

Wilson, John F. *Public Religion in American Culture.* Philadelphia: Temple University Press, 1979.

Wilson, John F. "Religion at the Core of American Culture." In *Altered Landscapes: Christianity in America,* 1935–85 (R. Handy Festschrift), D. Lotz, D. Shiver, and J. Wilson, eds. Grand Rapids: Wm. B. Eerdmans Publishing Co., 1989, pp. 362-76.

Wilson-Kastner, Patricia. *Faith, Feminism, and the Christ.* Philadelphia: Fortress Press, 1983.

Wright, Conrad. "The Growth of Denominational Bureaucracies: A Neglected Aspect of American Church History." *Harvard Theological Review* 77 (1984): 177-94.

Wuthnow, Robert. *The Restructuring of American Religion: Society and Faith Since World War II.* Princeton: Princeton University Press, 1988.

———. *The Struggle for America's Soul: Evangelicals, Liberals, and Secularism.* Grand Rapids: Wm. B. Eerdmans Publishing Co., 1989.

The Church Confident

"Christianity can repent, but it must not whimper."

Charles Clayton Morrison
Lyman Beecher Lecturer, 1939